ENDANGERED

DATE DUE

JOHANN CHRISTOPH ARNOLD

ENDANGERED

Your Child

in a Hostile World

PLOUGH PUBLISHING HOUSE

In recognition of the child-centered vision this book promotes, Community Playthings and Rifton Equipment have chosen to sponsor its distribution to early childhood educators. For discounts on bulk orders, call Plough /USA at 1-800-521-8011 or 724-329-1100, or Plough/UK at 0800 018 0799 or 44 (0) 1580 88 33 44

COVER PHOTO: ©MIKE KRIETER /ZEPHYR IMAGES
A catalog record for this book is available from the British library

Library of Congress Cataloging-in-Publication Data

Arnold, Johann Christoph, 1940-
   Endangered : your child in a hostile world / Johann Christoph Arnold.
     p. cm.
Includes index.
   ISBN 0-87486-997-8 (pbk. : alk. paper)
   1. Children – Social conditions. 2. Parent and child. 3. Child
welfare. 4. Child consumers. I. Title.
   HQ767.9 .A76 2000
   305.23 – dc21

                        00-009440

PRINTED IN CANADA

"Whenever people ask me about having children or not having children, I never tell them what to do," Morrie said, looking at a photo of his oldest son. "I simply say, 'There is no experience like having children.' That's all. There is no substitute for it. You cannot do it with a friend. You cannot do it with a lover. If you want the experience of having complete responsibility for another human being, and to learn how to love and bond in the deepest way, then you should have children." "So would you do it again?" I asked. "Would I do it again?" he said to me, looking surprised. "Mitch, I would not have missed that experience for anything…"

Mitch Albom
from *Tuesdays with Morrie*

To my grandparents,
Eberhard and Emmy Arnold,
whose life-long love
of children and young people
inspired this book.

Contents

Foreword

Hope is the thing left to us in a bad time.

IRISH PROVERB

There are more than enough books on parenting. That was one of the few things I was certain of when I set out to write this book. A father of eight and grandfather of twenty-two, I have had ample opportunities to experience parenting in action, and I sense that what today's parents lack most is not expertise or ideas, but daring. They simply lack the courage to put their children first.

As we enter a new millennium, we stand at a crossroads. On the one hand, prosperity and progress have benefited many; on the other, millions are trapped in situations of homelessness and unemployment, starvation and disease. The split is not only an economic one. Evils such as racism, violence, and neglect affect people on both sides of the divide. Only a few weeks ago, a prominent West Indian journalist in New York City wrote of his concern over relations between his city's police force and non-whites like himself: "My son is an endangered species every time he walks outside."

In general, the forces that transformed society so rapidly over the last generation continue to change it at such a rate that it is anyone's guess what the world will look like in even a decade or two. But one would have to be extremely naive to predict that it will be a safer or happier place for children.

A book on parenting can't change the world. But parents and teachers can – by saving each child entrusted to them. And that's why I have decided, in this book, to offer you the encouragement of others who have "been there." Whether single, married, or divorced, whether comfortable or struggling, these people have children of their own or work with children, and the wisdom reflected in their stories is rooted in the realities of daily life. But it is also born of hope. Because no matter how dark the horizon seems, we must never forget that for us, as for children, a new millennium – and the chance for a new start – begins every morning.

Rifton, New York
May 2000

1. The Trap of Indifference

The greatest evil in the world is not anger or hatred, but indifference.

ELIE WIESEL

When Susan and Nick decided to start a family, they were both working full-time jobs, but try as they might, their combined income simply "didn't go the whole distance." Savings were out of the question – after the bills were paid, there was never enough to put anything aside. On top of that, Nick's job carried no medical insurance, and Susan's no maternity leave. Still, they were determined to have a baby. So they did.

Not surprisingly the couple found little sympathy at work. Nick describes himself as "just a regular family man working hard," but says he was treated "like a welfare cheat." As for Susan, she was asked, "Couldn't you have planned a little further ahead?" No one was openly cruel, but no one was happy for them either, and as time went on, this indifference came to hurt more deeply than anything that might have been said.

When the baby came, the couple delighted in their new role as parents, but barely. There wasn't any time. For one thing, delivery room complications resulted in unexpected medical bills, and Susan had to get back to work right away. For another, it was almost impossible to find affordable day care on the couple's newly constrained budget. After a frantic two-week search, Nick found a place that had an opening for newborns, but when he went to view the place, he found a private residence owned by two elderly women, and some eighteen babies and toddlers, each dirtier and more disconsolate than the rest, strapped into car seats and watching television. Susan hated the place as much as Nick did, but there was little choice. Drop the job, or enroll baby Jenny. They did the latter.

Susan and Nick's dilemma is not an unusual one; in fact, it is repeated in countless places and variations. But its familiarity makes it no less shameful or frustrating. When a young couple who wishes to start a family faces such obstacles in one of the most prosperous countries in the world – and one of the most prosperous decades in memory – something is seriously wrong. And I'm not talking about a lack of planning.

On the bright side, of course, Jenny is better off than many children: born to a mother who wants her, she also has a father and a roof over her head. But what kind of world awaits her as she grows?

Each day in America, some 22 children are murdered or killed; each night an estimated 100,000 children go to sleep in parks, under bridges, or in homeless shelters. Some 2,800 children see their parents divorce each day, while for a 1.5 million, the only way to see their fathers is to visit them in prison.

Globally, the statistics are even more unimaginable: almost 40,000 children starve to death daily, while millions more work under forced labor conditions, including the brothels of Asia's tourist-supported sex market. In armed conflicts from Central America to Africa, an estimated quarter of a million children are currently employed as soldiers, some of them as young as five years of age.

For Jenny, as for countless other children, the world is hardly a welcoming place. From the playground to the bedroom, the issues that will sooner or later confront them read like items from a police blotter: child abandonment and child abuse, sexual assault and self-mutilation, exposure to drugs and easy access to guns. What's a parent to do?

It's a good question. Most of us have our hands full just looking out for our own children without worrying about someone else's day care problems – let alone the nameless masses of Mozambique, Sao Paulo, Calcutta, or the Bronx. With only so many hours in the day, we have our own lives to live, and when the chips are down, it's clear who's going to get our attention first. Of course, that's precisely the point of my anecdote about Susan and Nick. Unable to fathom more than the most immediate needs, even for the best reasons, we try to cope by blocking out the rest. We end up caught in the trap of indifference.

As for statistics: the numbers are horrendous, but they're also mind-boggling, and even if we'd prefer not to admit it, they tend to overwhelm or bore rather than shock. Take, for example, the complete absence of any public outcry whatsoever when (on a *60 Minutes* segment in 1998) a reporter asked U.S. Secretary of State Madeleine Albright if she felt that UN-imposed sanctions on Iraq were "worth the price." After conceding that an estimated 750,000 children had died in the previous eight years as a direct result of those sanctions, she said, "We feel that this is a hard choice, but we think – we think the price is worth it." Albright, a former war refugee, is also a mother, and I can hardly believe that she is truly as cold-hearted as this statement makes her sound. Still, if such a sentiment were only an expression of government policy and not a reflection of popular opinion, I think the sanctions in question would have been lifted long ago. In other words, I'm not sure Albright's statement can be explained away as a merely political ploy.

Ironically, at the same time that Washington was justifying the continued starvation of Iraq, it was also announcing plans to welcome the new millennium by proclaiming 2000 the Year of the Child. Incredulous, I wrote to African-American journalist Mumia Abu-Jamal, a friend, and asked him what he thought about it.

> I see nothing harmful in proclaiming a year of the child. Perhaps there is even something laudatory about it. But in truth such a proclamation, no matter how nobly-intentioned, will have little real impact on the wretched lives lived by billions of babies who fight to draw breath on this planet.
>
> Diplomats and politicians answer to power interests, and they are instruments of such forces. Last time I checked, kids don't have a PAC [political action committee], nor do they command capital. They are smooth little symbols that are kissed at election time. But when the real business of politics shifts into gear, they are virtually ignored.
>
> If they survive, today's children will inherit a world that their fathers and grandfathers have ravaged, where the seas are acidic cesspools that the whales have fled, where rain forests are Indian memories never to return, and where human

greed has plundered Mother Earth's innards and turned human genes into factories for profit. They will inherit a diminished planet where fresh water is increasingly rare, and where fresh air is a commodity...

We live in a world that fears and hates its young. How else can one explain the bequest of such a foul, polluted, and hollow inheritance? This generation, which came of age in the midst of a rising tide of human liberation movements, is now one of the most repressive in human history, as it consigns its young to more dungeons for longer periods than did their parents' generation. It bleeds resources from already crumbling urban and rural schools, and aids and abets an irrelevant education whose core message is obedience.

Knowledge is but another commodity that is available to the few that can afford it. For millions of poor children in a nation that has amassed more wealth than the ancient Roman Empire, schools are dreary and dilapidated – grim abattoirs of the mind.

Our children hunger for love. They have two-hundred-dollar sneakers, video games, computers. Some even have their own cars – the bright glittering detritus of two working parents. They have all of the latest toys, but no love.

Unloved, how can children love? Unloved, how can they do else than hate…

On calendars, in newspapers, and on the lying lips of pimping politicians, The Year of the Child will be proclaimed loudly and proudly. But after the calendar turns, the newspapers are balled up and trashed, and the politicians cry crocodile tears as they "feel your pain," our children will still be the castaways of the ship of capital. They are drowning in a sea of lovelessness, and after 2000 they will continue to drown.

Naturally we cannot only blame the government. We bear a guilt too, we whose privileged middle-class lifestyles have, at least in part, created the ghettos and barrios where every card is stacked against the children of the poor; who remain silent in the face of policies that threaten the future of whole nations; who look the other way when the children of other races and classes are repressed, imprisoned, starved, or enslaved. As long as we remain knowingly aloof, we cannot claim innocence.

To be charitable, many people are not so indifferent to the plight of the world's needy children as ignorant of it. That was certainly the case with me, at least until May 1998, when my church in upstate New York sent me to Baghdad. There I saw suffering on a scale I never could have imagined.

A good-will gesture by a group of Europeans and Americans opposed to the UN sanctions on Iraq, our journey included stops at bomb shelters, hospitals, nurseries, and schools and brought us face to face with some of the hardest sights I have ever seen: hundreds of starving children dying before our eyes, while weeping mothers begged us to tell them why "we" were doing this to them? Though tempted to explain that we were there in protest of our country's policies toward them, I found myself in tears instead. Unable to speak, I tried to comfort them by listening.

Since then my wife and I (and others from our church) have returned to Baghdad twice, bringing food, medications, and supplies, and offering our services in hospitals where the wards have not been cleaned for years.

Though a drop in the bucket in terms of their effectiveness, these trips were vital experiences for me, not least because they drove home a truth none of us can be reminded of often enough: it is always children who suffer most for the sins of the world. And that is as true in a "developed" country as in an impoverished or war-torn one.

Clearly we cannot all fly to Iraq or move to the inner city. Even if we could, there would be little purpose in doing so. But neither can it be right to close out everything that lies beyond our door – and settle for a life of self-centered oblivion.

Thoreau wrote in his journal, "Only that day dawns to which we are awake." It is the same with many of life's riddles. Once we get out of our easy chairs and open the blinds, their elusive answers will dawn on us. We will discern priorities that pull us beyond our comfort zones and into problems we can actually do something about. And we will realize how many children there are who can be reached and saved.

But that will mean putting away our speeches about the Year of the Child and finding the child who needs us today. It will mean laying aside our analyses about the endangered state of childhood and concerning ourselves with children themselves. It will mean starting to live as if children really mattered to us.

In 1991, while we spent billions to "save" the people of Kuwait from Iraq, two million of our own neglected children – three times Kuwait's entire population – attempted suicide. Eight years later, in 1999, we tried to "rescue" the people of Kosovo from Serbia by bombing both to smithereens; meanwhile, during the very same period, thousands of American and Western European children died at the hands of their own violent parents and guardians.

If children mattered to us, we would recognize that they are the real victims we ought to be fighting for and mobilize on their behalf. We would turn our national budget upside down, with spending for children at the top, and guns and bombs at the bottom – if we left them there at all. New schools, not new prisons, would mushroom across the land, and politicians would win on the most creative platform for education, not the toughest approach to dealing with crime.

If children mattered, our cities would be putting dollars into affordable day care and after-school programs, not instituting curfews and hiring cops. And they certainly would not hire officers like the one I recently read of, who caught the main dealer of a teenage drug ring in the act. Asked whether one successful arrest would really do any good, he replied, "No." What would? Curling his fingers to form the shape of a gun, he cocked his hand and said, "If I could shoot them as I caught them."

Call it a bad joke. Whatever it is, it's not a rare attitude. In a culture where violence – including violence against children – has become the stuff of everyday life, compassion has gone cold and the only thing left is such callousness.

Or is it? Uncaring employers and gun-toting policemen aside, new children are born into our torn and twisted world every day, and each one brings (in the words of Indian poet Tagore) the "renewed message that God has not lost faith in mankind." It's a mystical thought, but it carries a challenge as well. If the Creator has not lost faith in our humanity, who are we to do so? The world may be in a sorry state, but that should not keep us from welcoming children – the messengers of its salvation. After all, if the cause of so much that is wrong is our own indifference, the path toward a solution cannot remain hidden for long. At least that's what Mumia Abu-Jamal thinks:

> If the greatest evil in the world is not anger or hatred, but indifference, then the opposite also holds true: the greatest love is the attention we pay to each other, and especially to our children. We serve children best simply by noticing them – by paying attention to them…

2. Material Child

Where your treasure is,
there will your heart be also.

JESUS OF NAZARETH

"Come in," said the professor.

John opened the door. Goatstroke was reading an academic journal. He gestured toward the wooden chair that faced his desk. John sat down silently and looked around the room, waiting for his mentor to finish...

John inhaled, painfully. "You know Martha – my wife – is pregnant again."

Goatstroke inclined his head slightly.

"So," said the professor, "I imagine you'll have it taken care of as soon as possible?"

"Martha wants to have the baby," John finished in a weak voice...

"Yes, but –" Goatstroke had to stop, to collect himself. "Listen," he said. "You have got to persuade her. If not for her career, then for yours... You have got to understand...this is your career, John. You must have your priorities in order... This is the kind of thing that separates the men from the boys..."

In a world where the dollar has cast its spell over every corner of public and private life, the most insidious danger to children may be the economic lens through which we view them. To see children as assets or investments is calculating enough, but given the number of conversations like the one above (from writer Martha Beck's recent memoir about having a baby at Harvard) it is clear that plenty of parents-to-be see them in less favorable terms: as burdens, risks, and liabilities. Clearly, we live in a culture that not only fails children at repeated turns of the road but is often openly contemptuous of them.

Ironically, the same materialism that breeds such hostility toward children also welcomes them with open arms when they have money to spend. Labor laws may have removed children from the workforce in the western world, but our generation has its own, equally effective form of enslavement: the discovery of the child as a consumer. As advertisers tap the bottomless pockets of adults whose money is fueling the most prosperous economy in the history of the world, they are discovering the most lucrative market of all: their little (and not so little) boys and girls. At once the easiest targets and the most persuasive wheedlers, today's children and teens have been successfully harnessed to pull their parents back to the mall week after week, month after month, and year after year.

Schools are no better. In increasing numbers of districts around the country, financial incentives such as new computers, sports equipment, and vending machines are being used to coax principals into signing deals with companies such as Channel One and Pepsi, who gain in return the exclusive right to market their wares to eager crowds at lunchtime and recess.

Despite the fact that millions around the globe grow up in acute poverty, most children in developed regions like western Europe and the United

States have far more than they need; we are raising a generation of what can only be called spoiled brats. Many parents are quick to blame the materialistic culture at large – for example, the steady diet of commercials and advertisements that children are exposed to daily – but as far as I can tell, the problem has other roots as well.

Pampered children are the product of pampered parents – parents who insist on getting their own way, and whose lives are structured around the illusion that instant gratification brings happiness. Children are spoiled not only by an overabundance of food, toys, clothing, and other material things. Many parents spoil them simply by giving in to their whims. While they are still in the playpen, this is bad enough, but as they grow older, the problem gets much worse. How many harried mothers spend all of their energy simply trying to keep up with their children's demands? And how many more give in to their children just to keep them quiet?

As a child of European immigrants who fled to South America during the Second World War, I grew up in what I now see was poverty. For the first several years of my life, we often ate only the bare minimum: cornmeal mush with molasses, or bread spread with lard and sprinkled with salt – something we regarded as a special treat. Yet, I would find it hard to imagine a happier childhood. Why? Because my parents gave us time and attention on a daily basis. No matter how hectic their schedule, for instance, they tried to eat breakfast with us before we went off to school each morning. They did this for over a decade, until my youngest sister (there were seven of us) graduated from high school.

The idea of a family meal at the beginning (or even end) of the day is seen as a luxury by most people today; even if they wish for it, conflicting schedules and long commutes make it impossible. But regardless of the reason, it is the children who lose out, and I am not convinced that it is always a matter of economic necessity. As often as not, the fractured hodge-podge of comings and goings that passes for family life in many homes seems to be the result of an insistence on maintaining a certain standard of material well-being.

Obviously, it is impossible to live without money and material goods, and every household must have its provider and its plans for the future. But ultimately it is the love we give our children, and not the material things, that will remain with them for life. And that is something we all too easily forget when the lure of a bigger paycheck, a better job, or a chance to make an extra buck comes our way. As Pat, a friend who spent most of her childhood following her father from one job opportunity to the next, recently wrote to me:

> Like most men of his generation, my father chose to immerse himself in his career. He was an officer in the air force. I can remember very vividly the occasions that he really took time to be with us. Because they were so few, each one was very special. We loved our father very much; he was so attentive and gentle when he was at home. At the time we didn't feel ignored; it seemed quite normal that he had to work every weekend or be away for a month to a year at a time. But now that I'm an adult I wonder what he sacrificed all that time for. A career? His country? Certainly not for the money. It strikes me as selfishness masked as duty. Yet I am sure that if my marriage had continued and my husband and I would have had children,

we would have done the very same thing. It's considered "normal" in middle and upper-middle-class families to put one's career first…

I see so many middle-class parents immerse themselves in their work. Working forty to sixty hours a week is an easier way to get immediate satisfaction than spending time with your kids. It's much easier to be part of a system with defined rules and objectives, and to succeed in a corporate environment, than to sort things out at home.

A common excuse is, "I'm working to put my child through college," or "I want to pay off my mortgage so I can leave something for my children." There's no doubt about it: it's much harder to give yourself and your time to your children than to work "for them," to amass money "for the future" – in effect, to buy your children's love. But they don't want an inheritance. They want you, and they want you now.

Pat aptly points out that children don't see material benefits in the same way adults do. To go back to my childhood in South America: I distinctly remember a North American visitor who fussed over me and my sisters and asked us if it was hard to live with so little. Looking up at the stranger, I wondered if he was crazy. Hard? What on earth did he mean? I thought I was living in paradise. It is easy for me now, as an adult, to understand his point of view, especially after having brought up my own children in the relative wealth of the United States. But at the same time I cannot forget that fifty years ago, from a different angle, I saw it as the sign of a weak mind.

Speaking of differences in perspective, I have been amazed to find, on my travels around the world, that in some of the most impoverished places on earth there is also the greatest devotion to children. Iraq, Chiapas, Cuba, and the West Bank boast none of the material advantages that we take for granted in the developed sectors of the West. Infant mortality rates are high, food is meager, and medicines are always in short supply, if they are available at all. Toys are sticks or tin cans; clothes are made of rags or old T-shirts; babies lack bottles and cribs and strollers. Yet nowhere have I seen such radiant smiles or such warmhearted hugs. Nowhere have I seen greater affection between parents and teens, elderly people and small children, than in these places.

In Havana, which I visited in 1997 with a group of

middle-school students from New York, I discovered the same thing. Living conditions in Cuba are not squalid, but the island still suffers from the economic chaos left by Russia's withdrawal at the end of the Cold War and from the harsh economic sanctions imposed by the United States. Buildings are crumbling, grocery and pharmacy shelves are bare, schools lack basic supplies, and public transport is unreliable. Yet again and again our group came across billboards and posters reminding passersby that "the children of Cuba are our first responsibility."

Cynics might interpret such signs as clever propaganda, but our experiences made it clear that this was not the case at all. On the contrary, we found the sentiments behind them at work in every classroom we visited: on the part of the students, a passion for learning and a healthy sense of self-esteem, and on the part of the teaching staff, a conviction that no matter how bad things get, the children must be cared for with love, pride, and respect. This was especially so in a hospital we visited that had taken in pediatric cancer patients from the Chernobyl region. The eagerness and joy of the children – as well as the quality of their care – is unforgettable.

What is it about the plush homes and classrooms of our own country, where every material need is more than adequately attended to, that leaves our children in such a different state? Perhaps, according to child psychiatrist Robert Coles, it is the lack of something to live and work for besides a better car and a bigger house:

> I think that what children...desperately need is a moral purpose, and a lot of our children here aren't getting that. Instead they're getting parents who are very concerned about getting them into the right colleges, buying the best clothes for them, giving them an opportunity to live in neighborhoods where they'll lead fine and affluent lives and where they can be given the best things, to go on interesting vacations, and all sorts of other things...

I don't advocate poverty. Nor am I blind to the fact that there are plenty of poor children in the "developed world," from the orchards of California and Washington to the slums of Rome and London's East End. In those places and others too numerous to name, children are being denied the most basic necessities – let alone the additional trappings that most of us feel we deserve. Yet I firmly believe that ultimately the well-being of a child is not dependent on his or her access to material wealth. Anyone who clings to such a short-sighted mentality has succumbed to a foolish and even dangerous myth.

Mother Teresa once observed, after a visit to North America, that she had never seen such an abundance of things. But, she went on, she had also never seen "such a poverty of the spirit, of loneliness, and of being unwanted...That is the worst disease in the world today, not tuberculosis or leprosy...It is the poverty born of a lack of love."

What does it mean to give a child love? Many parents, especially those whose work keeps them away from their families for days or even weeks at a time, try to overcome feelings of guilt by bringing home gifts. Well-meaning as they are, they forget that what their children really want, and need, is time and attentiveness, a listening ear and an encouraging word. Unfortunately, many children rarely receive these things.

When Gina, a friend of one of my daughters, took a job as a preschool teacher at a private day school in

Georgia, she was initially impressed. It was small, orderly, and well-furnished, with only a handful of children in each class, and all of them seemed to come from affluent homes. Before long, however, her enthusiasm turned to shock.

> The parents of the children I care for have everything they want – fancy cars, expensive clothes, big houses, and plenty to spend – but so many of them are going through divorces, so many are cheating, doing drugs and alcohol, or fighting and abusing each other at home...And you can see it in the kids.
>
> One little girl, Amanda, is three years old and seems to do nothing but throw temper tantrums – she has built up that much anger and frustration toward her parents. Often she says things like, "I hate Daddy" or "I'm not going to let my Mommy pick me up today."
>
> Amanda's parents don't live together; in fact, they've never been married. They have split custody, which means in her case that she spends a certain number of days per week with one parent, and then an equal number with the other, and so on. The days she gets switched from Daddy to Mommy and vice versa are always a mess. She wets

her bed at naptime, bites, hits, and scratches other kids, and generally disrupts the class at every opportunity.

Amanda's mother recently started going out with another guy, whom she has instructed Amanda to call "Dad," so now she has two Daddies. She's totally confused! On top of this, her mother expects her to be a "good girl" and look nice all the time. I've learned to make sure her hair isn't messy when her mother comes to get her at the end of the day.

There's another kid, Jared, who is extremely insecure, especially at naptime. Every day I have to sit next to his mat and rub his back or stroke his hair and sing to him – and that's not to get him to sleep, but just to calm him enough so he'll stay lying down.

I've been a sitter for Jared at home on occasion, and I can tell you why he's so unhappy – I found out the first evening I walked into the house. While his mother and dad rushed around their condo, fixing themselves up for a night out, ten-month-old baby Drew was sitting alone in his high chair in the kitchen with an empty bottle, crying. Jared, who's barely three, was alone in the living room, huddled on the sofa and watching an R-rated film on TV. As I stood there in the doorway, Jared's mother breezed past me with instructions about bedtimes before dashing off to some party with her husband, who was waiting outside in the car...

Clearly, it is one thing to have children. To create a home – a place of love and security – is quite a different matter. Unfortunately, many adults lack a sense of what this means. They are always "too busy" to have time for their children. Some parents are so pre-occupied with their jobs or (as in the case of the couple above) their leisure activities, that even when they do see their children at the end of a long day, they have no energy to really be there for them. They may sit in the same room – even on the same sofa – but their minds are still at work and their eyes on the evening news.

Deep down, every parent knows that bringing up a child entails more than providing for them. It's a rare father or mother who won't readily admit that they "really ought to spend more time" with their children. Yet it's just as rare to find parents who are willing not only to make such a recognition, but also to carry their good intentions into deeds.

Dale, a good friend who used to work for one of the largest law firms in the world, is one such parent. Though Dale once made more money per year than many people make in a lifetime, his paycheck and his prestige meant little to his family – perhaps because he was never at home to enjoy it with them. Excuses didn't go over well, either with his wife or his children, so rather than dig in his heels, Dale decided to try listening. Soon he had heard enough and made up his mind that there was only one thing to do: quit the firm.

> About ten years ago, a colleague and I were driving home from a Cub Scout pinewood derby competition…While the van-full of boys played and laughed in the back seats, he cleared his throat and broached a difficult subject. "Dale, you are making a big mistake by leaving the law firm. Do you realize that?" He was referring to my decision to give six months notice of my resignation. "It's not like you can just do whatever you want," he continued. "You have five children. You have a duty to give them the best life possible and to send

them to the best universities they can get into. You are shirking your duty."

I let a few moments pass. Finally, I replied. "It wasn't my idea. I never intended to cut back to less than twenty hours per week. My daughters pleaded that I quit."

It was true. For the last two years I had balanced twenty hours per week as a lawyer with an equal amount of time serving men dying of AIDS and cancer. This was a dramatic change from my life as a lawyer who lived on airplanes, opening accounts all over the country and working eighty to ninety hours a week. But then the Gulf War hit. My part-time legal work suddenly exploded, and soon I was back to my old schedule.

About six weeks into this reversion, my sixth grade daughter disappeared from school: she simply wasn't there one afternoon when we went to pick her up. We looked for her for over two hours and finally contacted the police. Later she was found by a friend walking alone on a roadside, crying. Her explanation was simple: "Dad, when you were gone all the time, it didn't matter. But now I've gotten used to you being here, and I can't take it. I want you to quit being a lawyer."

First I tried to get my ninth grade daughter to

talk some sense into her younger sister, but it
didn't work. She agreed with her completely. Then
I put it all down on paper for them to contem-
plate – to show them just how stiff the economic
consequences would be: pay for your own clothes,
car, gas, insurance, yearbooks, prom, college, trips,
etc. It didn't matter. My daughters wanted me…

My colleague was bringing the van to a stop at a
red light. "Look," he said impatiently. "You're
shirking your responsibility!" A few moments
passed before I sealed the discussion. It seemed
too important to finish quickly. I was focusing on
a clump of trees that refused to fall in line, refused
to be controlled, refused to be cut down and pro-
cessed at the corporate mill.

"I disagree," I told him gently. "I disagree. And
I bet, in your heart of hearts, that you do, too."

3. Great Expectations

*I have always been regretting that I
was not as wise as the day I was born.*

HENRY DAVID THOREAU

In a magazine piece I recently read about a Kenyan school that holds its classes in a shady grove outdoors, the headmaster (who had helped plant the trees as a child) recalled an African saying: "When you plant a tree, never plant only one. Plant three – one for shade, one for fruit, and one for beauty." On a continent where heat and drought make every tree valuable, that's wise advice. It's an intriguing educational insight too, especially in a time like ours, when vast numbers of children are endangered by a one-sided approach that sees them solely in terms of their ability to be fruitful – that is, to "achieve" and "succeed."

The pressure to excel is transforming childhood as never before. Naturally, parents have always wanted their children to "do well," both academically and socially. No one wants their child to be the slowest in the class, the last to be picked for a game on the field. But what is it about the culture we live in that has made that natural worry into such an obsessive fear, and what is it doing to our children? What is achievement, anyway? And what is success, other than some vague, lofty ideal?

My mother used to say that education begins in the cradle, and not one of today's gurus would disagree. But the differences in their approach are instructive. Whereas women of her generation sang their babies to sleep just as their mothers had done – because a baby loves the sound of its mother's voice – today's tend to cite studies on the positive effects of Mozart on the development of the infant brain. Fifty years ago, women nursed their babies and taught their toddlers finger games as a matter of course; today, most do neither, despite endless chatter about the importance of bonding and nurture.

As an author I became aware, after completing my first book, of something I had never noticed previously: the importance of white space. White space is the room between the lines of type, the margins, extra space at the beginning of a chapter, a page left blank at the beginning of the book. It allows the type to "breathe" and gives the eye a place to rest. White space is not something you're conscious of when you read a book. It is what isn't there. But if it were gone, you'd notice it right away. It is the key to a well-designed page.

Just as books require white space, so do children. That is, they need room to grow. Unfortunately, too many children aren't getting that. In the same way that we tend to overwhelm them with material things, we tend to over-stimulate and over-steer. We deny them the time, space, and flexibility they need to develop at their own pace.

The ancient Chinese philosopher Lao-Tzu reminds us that "it is not the clay the potter throws that gives the jar its usefulness, but the space within." Children need stimulation and guidance, but they also need time to themselves. Hours spent alone in daydreams or in quiet, unstructured activities instill a sense of security and independence and provide a necessary lull in the rhythm of the day. Children thrive on silence too. Without external distractions they will often become so consumed by what they are doing that they will be totally oblivious of everything around them. Unfortunately, silence is such a luxury that they are rarely allowed the opportunity for such undisturbed concentration. Whatever the setting – mall, elevator, restaurant, or car – the low murmur (or blare) of piped-in music or background noise is incessantly there.

As for the importance of giving children unstructured time, nineteenth-century writer Johann Christoph Blumhardt warns against the temptation to constantly intrude, and emphasizes the value of spontaneous activity: "That is their first school; they are teaching themselves, as it were. I often have the feeling that angels are around children…and that whoever is so clumsy as to disturb a child provokes his angel." Certainly there is nothing wrong with giving a child chores and requiring him to carry them out on a daily basis. But the way many parents over-book their children, emotionally and timewise, robs them of the scope they need to develop on their own.

It is a beautiful thing to see a child thoroughly absorbed in his play; in fact, it is hard to think of a purer, more spiritual activity. Play brings joy, contentment, and detachment from the troubles of the day. And especially nowadays, in our hectic, time- and money-driven culture, the importance of those things for every child cannot be emphasized enough. Educator Friedrich Froebel, the father of the modern kindergarten, goes so far as to say that "a child who plays thoroughly and perseveringly, until physical fatigue forbids, will be a determined adult, capable of self-sacrifice both for his own welfare and that of others." In an age when fears of playground injuries and the misguided idea that play interferes with "real" learning has led some forty percent of the school districts across the country to do away with recess, one can only hope that the wisdom of these words will not go entirely unheeded.

Allowing children the room to grow at their own pace does not mean ignoring them. Clearly, the bedrock of their security from day to day is the knowledge that we who care for them are always at hand, ready to help them, to talk with them, to give them what they need, and simply to "be there" for them. But how often are we swayed instead by our own ideas of what they want or need?

After the massacre at Columbine High School in April 1999, administrators rushed to provide psychologists and counselors to help traumatized students process their grief. But the teenagers didn't want to see experts. Though many privately sought professional help later, on their own terms, they first flocked to local churches and youth centers, where they dealt with their grief by talking to their peers.

The tendency to intervene, especially when a child is in trouble, is a natural one, but even then (perhaps especially then) it is vital to be sensitive to the child's needs. That's what Nicole, a mother of four, learned when their quiet English village was rocked by a savage murder:

> In June 1996 a local woman and her daughter were beaten to death near the edge of our property, while walking home from the local elementary school. A second daughter was beaten too, though

she survived. My daughters, who were six and eight, had often played with the girls, who were the same age. Days and nights of tears followed – in fact, my daughters still wept at intervals months after the incident.

As a mother, I was naturally worried about the traumatic effects of the crime, and the whereabouts of the murderer (who is still at large). I was tempted to question my children as to how they were doing and what they were thinking about the whole thing. But I tried to refrain. I knew that to help them, I needed to hear what they had to say – what their own spontaneous reactions were – and not impose or project my own motherly ideas on them first...

Amazingly, they never spoke once in fear of our neighbors' murderer, as every adult in the area was doing. Instead, they asked, "Why did that man hate them so much? They didn't do anything to him..."

In the weeks after the murder, well-meaning friends repeatedly urged us to "move on." "Don't let your children get hung up on this gruesome event," they warned us. "Help them get over it as quickly as possible." But I couldn't. At that point my children needed to grieve, and I could not bring myself to subject them to adult ideas about healing.

In *Ordinary Resurrections,* his new book about children in the South Bronx, Jonathan Kozol reflects on another angle of the same issue: the way adults tend to guide children through even the most casual conversations. He says it, too, is a result of our tendency to hurry – and our reluctance to let them sort life out in their own way, at their own pace.

> Children pause a lot when reaching for ideas. They get distracted. They meander – blissfully, it seems – through acres of magnificent irrelevance. We think we know the way they're heading in a conversation, and we get impatient, like a traveler who wants to "cut the travel time." We want to get there quicker. It does speed up the pace of things, but it can also change the destination.

Of all the ways in which we push children to meet adult expectations, the trend toward high-pressure academics may be the most widespread, and the worst. I say "worst" because of the age at which children begin to be subjected to it, and the fact that for some of them school quickly becomes a place they dread, and a source of misery they cannot escape for months at a time.

As someone whose scholastic career included plenty of mediocre grades, I am familiar enough with the dread that accompanies bringing home a report card. Thankfully, my parents cared far more about whether I got along with my peers than whether I achieved an A or a B. Even when I failed a class, they refrained from scolding me, and eased my anxieties by assuring me that there was a lot more in my head than I or my teachers realized; it just hadn't come to the surface yet. According to Melinda, a veteran preschool teacher in California, such encouragement is only a dream for many children, especially in homes where academic failure is seen as unacceptable.

> We have parents asking whether their two-and-a-half-year-olds are learning to read yet, and grumbling if they can't. The pressure some parents put on children is just incredible. I see children literally shaking and crying because they don't want to go in to testing. I've even seen parents dragging their child into the room...
>
> I had a little boy one year, Miles, whose parents were pushing him to get him ready to enter a very expensive private school. I bumped into his father at the beginning of the next school year and he

said, "You know, Miles has been so stressed out
that we're going to get him into counseling." It
was true that Miles was stressed out, but I was sure
it was because of the rigorous testing they'd put
him through during the summer…He had started
crying the day of the testing, and he'd cried every
day since then.

In some instances, the frenzy to compete begins even
before a child is ready to start school, as this recent
newspaper column about the trials of one New York
City couple shows:

A couple of weeks ago, she and her husband got
word that their five-year-old son had been skunked
at all six private schools they applied to for next
fall's kindergarten class. "Don't worry," the head
of their nursery school had assured them. "You will
certainly get into at least one of your top choices."

Famous last words. For whatever reasons, all
six schools passed on their bright son with the
winning smile and splendid test scores. That tattoo
of rejection hurt, she admits. Nor did it help to
learn that other families landed in the same boat.

Now comes the hard part…Do they move, re-
luctantly, out of town? Do they keep their son in
nursery school for now and try the private-school

rat race again next year? Do they sigh in resignation and send him to the local public school?

The dilemma facing this couple is a measure of how frantic life has become...in a world of strivers. "People are twisting themselves inside out," the woman said. "You slap yourself around and say, 'It's only kindergarten.' We're not talking about cancer. But it changes your life...Besides," she added, "the parental community can be vicious... Your child's admissions profile becomes a measure of your success. That's the yuckiest part of it. These are babies we're talking about."

In the end, she said, she and her husband will probably keep their son in his present nursery and then go through the private-school drill once more, next year. "That's what tears me up," she said. "He has to be paraded like a show horse again."

It's true the examples above represent the extreme end of the spectrum. Still, they cannot be dismissed, because they shed light on a disturbing trend that affects education at all levels. More and more, it seems that we have lost sight of the "child" in childhood and turned it into a joyless training camp for the adult world. Jonathan Kozol writes:

From around the age of six or seven, and up to eleven or maybe twelve, the gentleness and honesty – the sweetness – of children is so apparent. Our society has missed an opportunity to seize that moment. It's almost as though we view those qualities as useless, as though we don't value children for their gentleness, but only as future economic units, as future workers, as future assets or deficits.

When you read political debates on how much we should spend on children, you'll notice that the argument usually has nothing to do with whether children deserve a gentle and happy childhood, but whether investment in their education will pay off economically twenty years later. I always think, why not invest in them simply because they're children and deserve to have some fun before they die? Why not invest in their gentle hearts as well as in their competitive skills?

The answer, of course, is that we have abandoned the idea of education as growth, and decided to see it only as a ticket to the job market. Guided by charts and graphs, and cheered on by experts, we have turned our backs on the value of uniqueness and creativity and fallen instead for the lie that the only way to measure a child's progress is a standardized test. Not only are we neglecting to plant trees for shade and beauty – we are planting for only one variety of fruit. Or, as Malvina Reynolds puts it in her song "Little Boxes":

> And they all play on the golf course,
>   and drink their martinis dry,
> And they all have pretty children,
>   and the children go to school,
> And the children go to summer camp,
>   and then to the university,
> Where they put them all in boxes,
>   and they come out all the same.

Granted, children ought to be stretched and intellectually stimulated. They should be taught to articulate their feelings, to write, to read, to develop and defend an idea; to think critically. But what is the purpose of the best academic education if it fails to prepare children for the "real" world beyond the confines of the classroom? What about those life-skills that can never be taught by putting a child on a bus and sending him to school?

As for the things that schools are supposed to teach, even they are not always passed on. Writer John Taylor Gatto points out that though American children sit through an average of 12,000 hours of compulsory academic instruction, there are plenty who leave the system as 17- and 18-year-olds who still can't read a book or calculate a batting average – let alone repair a faucet or change a flat.

It is not just schools that are pressuring children into growing up too fast. The practice of rushing children into adulthood is so widely accepted and so thoroughly ingrained that people often go blank when you voice your concern about the matter. Take, for example, the number of parents who tie up their children's after-school hours in extracurricular activities. On the surface, the explosion of opportunities for "growth" in things like music and sports might look like the perfect answer to the boredom faced by millions of latchkey children. But the reality is not always so pretty. Tom, an acquaintance with friends in suburban Baltimore, says:

> It's one thing when a child picks up a hobby, a sport, or an instrument on her own steam, but quite another when the driving force is a parent with an overly competitive edge. In one family I know – I'll call them the Joneses – Sarah showed a

genuine talent for the piano in the second grade, but by the time she was in the sixth, she wouldn't touch a keyboard for any amount of coaxing. She was tired of the attention, sick of lessons (her father was always reminding her what a privilege they were), and virtually traumatized by the strain of having been pushed through one competition after another. Yes, Sarah played Bach beautifully at seven. But at ten she was interested in other things.

In the case above, and countless others, the pattern is all too familiar: ambitious expectations are followed by the pressure to meet them, and what was once a perfectly happy part of a child's life becomes a burden that is impossible to bear.

Einstein once wrote that if you want brilliant children, read them fairy tales. "And if you want them to be more brilliant, read them more fairy tales." Obviously, such a quip is not the sort of answer an expert might give to the discouraging trends described above. But I still believe it is a thought worth reflecting on. It is the inventive sort of wisdom without which we will never pull ourselves out of the ruts we are currently stuck in.

As for the parental desire to have brilliant children in the first place, it is surely just another sign of our distorted vision – a reflection of the way we tend to view children as little adults, no matter how loudly we may protest such a "Victorian" idea. And the best antidote to that is to drop all of our adult expectations entirely, to get down on the same level as our children, to look them in the eye. Only then will we begin to hear what they are saying, to find out what they are thinking, and to see the goals we have set for them from their point of view. Only then will we be able to lay aside our ambitions and recognize, as poet Jane Tyson Clement puts it:

> child, though I am meant to teach you much,
> what is it, in the end,
> except that together we are
> meant to be children
> of the same Father,
> and I must unlearn
> all the adult structure
> and the cumbering years
> and you must teach me
> to look at the earth and the heaven
> with your fresh wonder.

"Unlearning" our adult mindsets is never easy, especially at the end of a long day, when children can sometimes seem more of a bother than a gift. When there are children around, things just don't always go as planned. Furniture gets scratched, flower beds trampled, new clothes torn or muddied, toys lost and broken. Children want to handle things and play with them. They want to have fun, to run in the aisles; they need space to be rambunctious and silly and noisy. After all, they are not china dolls or little adults, but unpredictable rascals with sticky fingers and runny noses who sometimes cry at night. Yet if we truly love them, we will welcome them as they are.

4. The Power of a Hug

Before I had children, I had six theories about bringing them up; now I have six children and no theories.

LORD ROCHESTER

Mention child rearing to Eric, and you're sure to get him going about his childhood. The third of eight siblings, he grew up in a well-heeled suburban neighborhood that regarded his family as a model household. A doctor and devoted family man, Eric's father returned from his office on time every evening and rarely went out on weekends. His stay-at-home mother was equally devoted. Yet neither Eric nor any of his brothers and sisters liked being at home, especially when their father was around.

Our household functioned wonderfully, but only by appearances. In actual fact it was ruled by fear. It's not that my father ever beat us – though he did on rare occasions spank or slap us. But woe betide you if you set him off. You never knew what kind of punishment you'd receive…

Dad, a master disciplinarian, kept us in line by effectively crippling us with an ongoing sense of dread. One summer night he caught my older brother Jack sneaking out of his bedroom window to go out with his friends. Dad ran outside and waited till he was safely on the ground. Then he confronted him: "Well, son, it's clear you prefer running around outside. Maybe you ought to stay outside."

For the rest of that summer Jack had to eat his meals outside, next to the dogs. "Maybe he'll learn what it's like to act as a civilized human being," Dad explained to us younger ones. Jack left home when he was sixteen and never came back.

Another time Dad grounded my older sister Mary, the family goody-goody, for a whole summer. Mary was normally super-responsible, but at the end of her sophomore year she skipped one class, and Dad snapped. I can still see her, talking through our backyard fence to her friends, day after day, week after week. It must have been the most humiliating punishment.

As for myself, there are numerous reasons why I was deathly afraid to cross Dad's path. But one example will suffice. It must have been when I was eleven or twelve – in the sixth grade – when I tried smoking for the first time and got caught. First I was sent to my room, where I waited for what seemed like hours. Then Dad came in. He advised me that I had two options. I could either smoke the entire pack I had started right away until they were all smoked, or display it on my window sill for a month and explain to everyone who came in – including my siblings and friends – why they were there, and how disgusting my father thought smoking was. I knew where the first option would lead – I would have been sick – so I decided on the second.

For the entire next month, I could think of only one thing: how to keep people from entering my bedroom. In fact, I literally feared cigarettes for years afterward. I was so afraid of smoking that whenever I walked down a street I made sure to keep clear of any and every cigarette butt on the ground. I was worried that Dad might drive by and think that I had been smoking.

One time my English class was assigned an essay for homework that I knew would require my writing the word "cigarette." I was so scared at the thought of what Dad might think that I destroyed the assignment and had to lie my way out of explaining why I didn't have it.

Something like cigarettes might seem like a small thing, but not for Dad...By the time I was in high school I had gone pretty much ballistic and did everything I could think of to spite him. He could have the final word at home, I said to myself, but nowhere else. I guess it goes without saying that we never had (and still don't have) any relationship worth speaking of.

Eric's story is a miserable one, but for countless adults it will ring a familiar bell: the memory of a similar incident that marred what could have been a happy childhood. Sadly, parents are sometimes so blinded by their principles that they are unable to follow their hearts. Ready to "do the right thing" at any cost, they are masters of their domain – but all too often they lose their children in the process.

Discipline is probably the most overused word in the vocabulary of parenting, and also the most misunderstood. Discipline is not just punishment. What is it then? It is guidance, but not control; persuasion, but not suppression or coercion. It may include punishment or the threat of punishment, but never cruelty or force. It should never mean the use of corporal punishment, something I feel is always a sign of moral bankruptcy. What it will always include is loving consideration for the inner disposition of the child. As my grandfather, writer Eberhard Arnold, put it, "That is the crucial element. Raising children should mean helping them to become what they already are in God's mind."

Thankfully, my siblings and I received such consideration from our parents throughout our upbringing, and the result was a relationship of mutual love and trust that lasted, unbroken, to the end of their lives. Of course, this relationship was grounded in plenty of old-fashioned discipline, including rows so loud and dramatic (especially if we talked back to our mother) that we would be shamefaced for hours afterwards, and certain that the neighbors had heard every word.

Name-calling and mockery were cardinal sins in our house. Like boys and girls anywhere, we sometimes made fun of adults whose peculiarities made them stick out, like Nicholas, a simple-minded neighbor who stuttered, and Gunther, a pedantic, extremely tall librarian at school. But even if our targets knew nothing of the clever ridicule that went on behind their backs, our parents failed to see any humor in it. They had a nose for cruelty wherever it was and would not tolerate it for a minute.

Still, their tempers never lasted for long, and even if a punishment was deserved, it was sometimes dispensed with in favor of a hug. One time when I was eight or nine, I angered my father so much that he threatened to spank me. As I waited for the first blow, I looked up at him and, before I knew what I was doing, blurted out, "Papa, I'm really sorry. Do what you have to do – but I know you still love me." To my astonishment, he leaned down, put his arms around me and said with a tenderness that came from the bottom of his heart: "Christoph, I forgive you." My apology had completely disarmed him. Because this incident made me realize how much my father loved me, it has always remained vivid in my

mind. It also taught me a lesson I have never forgotten – one I drew on in dealing with my own children
years later: Don't be afraid to discipline a child, but
the moment you feel he is sorry, be sure there is
immediate and complete forgiveness on your part.

How different the landscape would look if each of
us were ready to practice such compassion – and not
just by hugging our own sons and daughters, but by
standing up for children everywhere! As it is, we are
bringing up a generation of children whom we not
only don't love, but fear. Signs of this are everywhere:
from nighttime curfews for urban youth in many big
cities to the criminalization of petty acts such as
"tagging" (graffiti-spraying), and the deployment of
armed guards and police officers at schools. Most
alarming of all are the skyrocketing rates of youth
incarceration.

Despite the obvious failure of such grim "solutions," attitudes toward young adults and children at
risk – and laws designed to seal their fate – grow
more repressive with every year. In California, legis-
lative initiatives like Proposition 21 have given un-
heard-of power to prosecutors in juvenile courts and
vastly increased the odds that suspects as young as

fourteen will be tried as adults. Meanwhile, in Texas, standardized reading tests taken by third graders are being used to project the number of new prison cells that will be needed by the time those children are adults (low scores are supposed to indicate a higher propensity for crime).

There's nothing new about using childhood personality traits to predict adult behavior; psychologists and psychiatrists have done it for decades. But what does it say about a society when its leaders bet on the failure of the next generation, and no one protests? What does it say about the way we view children, when we allow the very guardians of their future to dream such fatalistic dreams?

Clearly, a satisfying exploration of such big questions is beyond the scope of this book. So is the discussion of many other issues that would need to be addressed beforehand, such as why so many young men behind bars had trouble in the classroom in the first place, and what sort of obstacles were blocking their progress then.

I am also hesitant, in these pages, to advise readers on how to guide and discipline the child within the home; after all, each one brings with him or her a unique set of strengths and weaknesses, promises and challenges, as does every parent. Perhaps it is best to follow the wisdom of Janusz Korczak (1878–1942), a remarkable Jewish pediatrician whose story I will tell later. He writes:

> You yourself are the child you must learn to know, rear, and above all enlighten. To demand that others should provide you with answers is like asking a strange woman to give birth to your baby. There are insights that can be born only of your own pain, and they are the most precious. Seek in your child the undiscovered part of yourself.

Speaking of insights "born of pain," my wife, Verena, and I gained several in the course of bringing up eight children. Like most parents, it is probably safe to say that there is plenty we would do differently if we had the chance to do it again. Sometimes we unfairly assumed bad motives; at other times we had the wool pulled over our eyes; one day we were too lenient; the next, too strict. Of course, we did learn several basic lessons as well.

When a child is conscious of having done something wrong, but there are no consequences, he learns that he can get away with it. It is a terrible thing for a child to get that message. With a younger one, the issue might seem unimportant; his misdeed may actually be small. But it can have repercussions far into the future. The old saying, "Little children, little problems; big children, big problems," is easy enough to dismiss, yet like most clichés, it contains a significant truth. A six-year-old may only snitch cookies; at sixteen he may be shoplifting. And while the will of a small child may be guided with relative ease, a rebellious teenager can only be reined in with the most strenuous effort.

Despite the need for consequences, they are not sufficient in themselves. Discipline entails more than catching a child in the act and punishing him. Far more important is nurturing his will for the good, which means supporting him whenever he chooses right over wrong – or, as my mother used to put it, "winning him for the good." Of course, such affirmation has nothing to do with manipulation; the purpose of rearing them can never be to simply make them obey. Rather, our goal should always be to help them toward the confidence that enables them to explore life and yet know their limits. That is the best preparation for adulthood.

Writer Anthony Bloom was once asked by an interviewer what it was about his upbringing that stood out most clearly to him as an adult. Bloom, the son of a famous diplomat whose travels took the family on colorful adventures all over the world, answered simply, "two things my father said, which impressed me and have stayed with me all my life."

> One was this: I remember he said after a holiday, "I worried about you," and I said, "Did you think I'd had an accident?" He said, "That would have meant nothing...I thought you had lost your integrity." Then on another occasion he said to me, "Always remember that whether you are alive or dead matters nothing. What matters is what you live for and what you are prepared to die for." These two things were the background of my education...

Unlike fathers such as Bloom's, who inspired integrity rather than tried to teach it, there are those parents who fall for the mean-spirited habit of trying to catch their child red-handed and then using their evidence to prove his guilt. That is an act of moral violence. So is distrusting a child, spying on him, or reading bad motives into his behavior, all of which will weaken him by making him doubt himself. Constantly criticizing and correcting a child will likewise discourage him. Worse, it will take away the best reason he has to trust in you: his confidence that you understand him. Froebel writes:

> Too many adults blame children who – though they may not be wholly innocent – are yet without guilt. That is, the children are unaware of the motives and incentives the adults accuse them of, which make their actions "bad." Children often receive punishment for things they have learned from these very adults...But that does nothing other than teach them new faults – or at very least bring to their attention ideas that might never have occurred to them on their own.

Naturally, every child needs correction regularly. Most need it several times daily. But when children are punished too harshly, the ultimate purpose of correcting them – helping them to make a fresh start – is overshadowed by the discipline itself. That is why it is always best to believe in the power of good and to give a child the benefit of doubt.

A fault like selfishness is rarely the same in children as in adults. Unable to see the world around them from anything but their own limited perspective, children feel fully in possession of it. Especially when small, they simply are – innocently and justifiably – the center of their own little universes.

Dishonesty is another issue parents tend to tackle with far too little regard for the child's point of view. It is surely important, when a child has been dishonest, to get to the facts of what happened and to encourage the child to face up to them. But it is rarely good to probe into the child's motives, and always wrong to push for a confession. After all, it may be nothing more than embarrassment or shame that caused the child to wriggle out of something by means of a half-truth to begin with, and if pressed, he may be so afraid of the consequences that he will tell an outright lie. Don't adults do that, too, for the very same reasons?

Forgiveness is necessary dozens of times a day. No matter how many times a child gets into trouble, never lose faith in him. As with lying, who is to say that any other fault a child must struggle to overcome does not reflect the same fault or tendency in his parents? To label a child as hopeless is to be tempted by despair, and to the extent that despair is a lack of hope, it is also a lack of love. If we truly love our children, we may at times throw up our hands in desperation, but we will never give up on them. God sent the Hebrews not only the Law of Moses but also manna, the bread of heaven. Without such bread – that is, without warmth, humor, kindness, and compassion – the most carefully considered discipline will eventually backfire.

There's no question that being a friend and companion as well as a parent requires double the patience and energy. But as Dale – the attorney who gave up his job to be a father – notes, there are few things as satisfying:

> When I think about it, it is much easier to live with children who fear you than it is to live with children who love you, because if your children fear you, when you come home they're gone. They scatter. They go to their rooms and shut the door, and you make it easier for them by piling their rooms full of computers, and TVs, and stereos, and everything else. But if you have children who love you, you can't get them out of your hair! They're hanging on to your legs, they're pulling

on your pants, you come home and they want your attention. You sit down, they're all over your lap. You feel like a walking jungle gym. You also feel loved.

The willingness to be vulnerable is an important part of parenting, too. For my wife and me, few experiences brought us as close to our children as the times we overreacted but then realized it and asked them to forgive us. If nothing else, it reminded us each time that just as we adults depend on the promise of being able to start over every morning, children do too. They should always be given the same chance, no matter how bad the previous day. And no matter what they are going through, they should always feel the assurance that we are ready to stand by them – not hovering over them, but at their side.

Obviously, every family has its ups and downs, its trying moments, its embarrassing dramas. There is nothing as emotionally complex as the relationship between a parent and a child. But there is also nothing as beautiful. And that is what we need to hold on to whenever we reach the end of our rope.

Earlier in this chapter I referred to Janusz Korczak, whose writings on children are revered throughout Europe. A teacher whose selfless devotion to orphans in the Warsaw Ghetto earned him the title King of Children, Korczak never tired of reminding people how it felt to be a child in an adult world and emphasizing the importance of educating children not "from the head" but "from the heart."

Korczak's insistence on what he called "standing with the child" was not only a principle. On August 6, 1942, as the two hundred orphans under his care were rounded up and loaded onto trains headed for the gas chambers of Treblinka, Korczak refused the last-minute offers of Gentile friends who arranged for his escape and chose instead to accompany his charges on the gruesome ride that carried them to their deaths.

Few stories of devotion are as stirring as Korczak's, and as surreal, perhaps because of the gulf between our circumstances and the unspeakable ones that necessitated his sacrifice. Yet despite the distance between his era and ours, far too many children in the world today suffer for want of even one such guardian – one adult who will take them by the hand and stick with them, come what may. And so for us, who live in a time of relative peace and prosperity, Korczak's last recorded words not only remind us of his heroism, but stand as a challenge to each of us who has ever raised – or hopes to raise – a child: "You do not leave sick children in the night," he said. "And you do not leave them in a time like this."

5. Deeds, Not Words

*Don't worry that your children
never listen to you. Worry that they
are always watching you.*

ROBERT FULGHUM

In a recent news article about high school students in Tokyo, the writer notes that though the stereotypical Japanese teen is obsessed with academic success, the reality is often quite different. "...In the last five years, freewheeling sex, heavy drinking and delinquency have exploded among the high-school set. In the place of the nose-to-the-grindstone ethic of long study hours and single-minded focus on

exams and careers…the motto of the current crop of
15- to 18-year-olds seems to be that girls and boys
just want to have fun."

While acknowledging the fact that some of the
more outrageous claims he heard may be exaggera-
tions – "We don't have any real serious boyfriends,
just sex friends," a group of girls told him – the
writer says that for many of the students he talked
to, daily life really is an endless cycle of shopping,
having sex, doing drugs, and visiting tanning salons.
Tired of incessant lectures about the virtues of indus-
triousness, alarming numbers are dropping out of
high school altogether and opting instead for the
"excitement" of urban nightlife.

"In an earlier generation, these children…might
have chosen to run away," a youth worker told the
reporter. "Nowadays, though, many parents avoid
involvement in the emotional conflicts of their teenage children – and runaways are few because the
household is so free…More and more, people are trying to enjoy their own lives, and they are gradually
becoming indifferent to their children." (Interestingly
enough, no parents are quoted in the article. Perhaps

they weren't available for interviews, or wouldn't talk. Either way, their children made it clear that they are not a very important part of their lives.)

To anyone out of touch with today's teens – not just in Tokyo, but in any large "westernized" city – such an attitude might seem shocking. Yet it shouldn't be. In a way, it is the logical outcome of a cultural environment built on the idea that the only worthy goal is doing well enough to make money and "have fun." Why bother with all the work if you can party now, at your parents' expense?

Ask any mother and father what they think about a trend like the one I've just described, and you'll get blank stares or defiant replies. "What do I think? It's outrageous. I'd never let my daughter..." Even the most dysfunctional parent knows, deep down, what's good or bad for a child. Unfortunately, there's a gulf between knowing what you want for a child, and being able to ensure that he or she acts accordingly. And it's clear that in many homes the gulf is not being bridged. Despite all the talk and all the nicely formulated values, the basic message is not getting through.

In the case of Tokyo's trend-setting teens, for instance, I am sure that their parents and teachers have made numerous appeals on behalf of their future, their health, their ability to contribute to society in a positive way. But I am also sure that their children aren't dumb. And as far as they can tell, what their parents really care about is their grades, not them. So they rebel.

As conventional wisdom goes, teenage angst is "just a phase." Adolescents have always chafed under parental authority, and they always will. When rebellion becomes a way of life, however, we cannot brush it off. We need to look a little deeper. What is it that today's children are rebelling against so vigorously, and why?

To me, the answer is simple: hypocrisy. The word is admittedly a strong one; it may even seem cruel to suggest that there are parents who consciously raise their children to act one way while simultaneously doing the opposite. But the hard truth is that this does happen – in far too many ways. Consider this anguished outpouring from a student at Texas A&M who felt compelled to explain, after the Columbine massacre, why she thought things had "become so bad":

> ...Let me tell you this: these questions don't represent only me but a whole generation that is struggling to grow up and make sense of this world. People may label us "Generation Next," but we are more appropriately "Generation Why?"
>
> Why did most of you lie when you made the vow of 'til death do us part?
>
> Why do you fool yourselves into believing that divorce really is better for the kids in the long run?
>
> Why do so many of you divorced parents spend more time with your new boyfriend or girlfriend than with your own children?
>
> Why did you ever fall victim to the notion that kids are just as well off being raised by a complete stranger at a day care center than by their own mother or father?
>
> Why do you look down on parents who decide to quit work and stay home to raise their children?
>
> Why do you allow us to watch violent movies but expect us to maintain some type of childlike innocence?
>
> Why do you allow us to spend unlimited amounts of time on the Internet but still are

shocked about our knowledge of how to build bombs?

Why are you so afraid to tell us "no" sometimes?

Call us what you want to, but you will be surprised how we will fail to fit into your neat little category...Now is the time to reap what you have sown. You might not think so, but I can guarantee that Littleton will look like a drop in the bucket compared to what might occur when a neglected "Generation Why?" comes to power.

Accusing as some of these questions may seem, I believe every one of them is valid, and vital for every parent to consider. Many of the issues they raise are too complex to answer in words alone, but they all touch on one central issue: the widespread perception of young adults that their elders are frauds.

Hypocrisy rears its head early in parenting, but it mostly appears in very subtle ways. Sometimes it is rooted in the confusion that arises when a child hears one thing at school and another at home; one direction from one parent, and a second from the other; one set of guidelines in one classroom, and an entirely different set in the next. In other instances, it stems from simple inconsistency: a child has just learned a lesson or a rule, only to find her parent breaking it, making an exception, or explaining it away. All this is usually harmless enough. It is part of life.

The real problem arises – and this is more widespread than one might think – when children are taught to "do as I say, not as I do." Told this half-jokingly in one situation after another, they gradually learn that there is never anything so black and white that is always good or bad, at least not until they make the wrong choice at the wrong time. When that happens, they get punished for their lapse of judgment. And they will always find the punishment unjust.

Being a father, I know how hard it is to be consistent – and conversely, how easy it is to send confusing signals without even realizing it. Having counseled hundreds of teenagers over the last three decades, I also know how sensitive young adults are to mixed messages and inconsistent boundaries, and how readily they will reject both as clear signs of parental hypocrisy. But I have also learned how quickly the worst family battle can be solved when parents are humble enough to admit that their expectations were unclear or unfair, and how quickly most children will respond and forgive.

Reflecting on the ways in which children so often mirror their parents – in actions, attitudes, behavioral characteristics, and personal traits – my grandfather writes that children are like barometers: that is, they visibly record whatever influences and pressures currently affect them, whether positive or negative. Happiness and security, generosity and optimism will often show themselves in children to the same degree that they are visible in their parents. It is the same with negative emotions. When children notice anger, fear, insecurity, or intolerance in an adult – especially if they are the target – it may not be long before they are acting out the same things.

In *The Brothers Karamazov*, Dostoyevsky's character Father Zossima reminds us that this sensitivity of children is so great that we may shape them without even knowing it, and he admonishes us to consider the effect of everything we say and do in their presence:

> Every day and hour...see that your image is a seemly one. You pass by a little child, you pass by spiteful, with ugly words, with wrathful heart; you may not have noticed the child, but he has seen

you, and your image, unseemly and ignoble, may remain in his defenseless heart. You don't know it, but you may have sown an evil seed in him, and it may grow...all because you did not foster in yourself an active, actively benevolent love.

Unlike the innocents of Dostoyesvky's time, children today are exposed to a steady barrage of images and expressions whose combined effect may be far greater than that of the most caring adult in their immediate lives. I am speaking, of course, of the news media, the entertainment industry, and the Internet, and the way in which they have replaced parents as the ultimate source of authority in millions of "wired" homes around the globe.

Parents can work themselves ragged trying to instill ideas of commitment and compassion, but as family expert Mary Pipher warns, TV – which tends to capture a child's undivided attention every time it is turned on, for as long as it is on – is a far more powerful parent. And if there's a conflict, there's little question who'll win: "This is the first time in the history of the human race that kids are learning how to behave from watching TV rather than from watching real people."

There is no question that every parent "tries hard" to raise good children. Given the state of our culture, which undercuts parents at every twist and turn, it's impossible to bring up any family at all without trying hard. But there's also no question that despite all our efforts, we are far from the models we ought to be. And that is the fault of every parent, not of some vague, dark power called Hollywood.

Take violence. Everyone is concerned about it, and everyone agrees it is bad for children. But what is anyone really doing about it? From the hallowed halls of Congress on down, precious little. Writing of the horror of Columbine, for instance, novelist Barbara Kingsolver observes that instead of coming to terms with the real forces that endanger children, we often trivialize them:

> In the aftermath of the high school killings in Littleton, Colorado, we have the spectacle of a nation acting baffled. Why would any student, however frustrated with mean-spirited tormentors, believe that guns and bombs are the answer?
>
> If we're really interested in this question, we might have started asking it awhile ago. Why does a nation persist in celebrating violence as an honor-

able expression of disapproval? In, oh let's say, Yugoslavia. Iraq. The Sudan. Waco – anywhere we get fed up with mean-spirited tormentors – why do we believe guns and bombs are the answer?

Let's not trivialize a horrible tragedy by pretending we can't make sense of it. "Senseless" sounds like "without cause," and requires no action. After an appropriate interval of dismayed hand-wringing, we can go back to business as usual. What takes guts is to own up: This event made perfect sense.

Children model the behavior of adults, on whatever scale is available to them. Ours are growing up in a nation whose most important, influential men – from presidents to film heroes – solve problems by killing people. It's utterly predictable that some boys who are desperate for admiration and influence will reach for guns and bombs. And it's not surprising that it happened in a middle-class neighborhood; institutional violence is right at home in the suburbs. Don't point too hard at the gangsta rap in your brother's house until you've examined the Pentagon in your own. The tragedy in Littleton grew straight out of a culture that is loudly and proudly rooting for the global shoot-out. That culture is us.

It may be perfectly clear to you that Nazis, the

Marines, "the Terminator," and the N.Y.P.D. all kill for different reasons. But as every parent knows, children are good at ignoring or seeing straight through subtleties we spin.

Here's what they see: Killing is an exalted tool for punishment and control. Americans who won't support it are ridiculed. Let's face it, though, most Americans believe bloodshed is necessary for preserving our way of life, even though this means we risk the occasional misfire – the civilians strafed, the innocent man wrongly condemned to death row.

If this is your position, I wonder if you'd be willing to go to Littleton and explain to some mothers about acceptable risk. In a society that embraces violence, this is what "our way of life" has come to mean. We have taught our children in a thousand ways, sometimes with flag-waving and sometimes with a laugh track, that the bad guy deserves to die...

Sound extreme? Don't kid yourself. Death is extreme, and the children are paying attention.

Clearly, the twisted way in which we deal with violence is not just a social or political phenomenon, but something that has roots in every living room. The issue here isn't just violence. No matter the vice or virtue, it is utterly futile to try to educate a child about it as long as our deeds and words remain at odds with each other.

Sex is another sphere where even the most well-meaning parents confuse children – if not with hypocrisy, then at very least with conflicting messages and confusing ideas. As with violence, so with sex: it's one of every parent's biggest concerns, and one of the most talked about. But amid all the worry about what to say to our sons and daughters, how to say it, and when, many of us are forgetting the most important thing: the power of our actions. Until we start living our convictions – until we demand of ourselves the same things we demand of our children – all our strenuous efforts at modeling integrity will fall flat.

Commenting on the age-old riddle of how to pass on one's values to the next generation, Blumhardt, the nineteenth-century pastor, admonishes religious parents for their tendency to moralize and preach, and criticizes their "illusions" about the value of rushing children to church. "As long as Christ lives only in your bibles...and not in your hearts," he says, "every effort to bring him to your children will fail." Regardless of one's faith, or whether one has a faith at all, the point is well made. Veteran civil-rights activist Assata Shakur writes:

> Your values must be real if you want to pass them down. It's too easy to engage in macho talk...and to forget about the ego and its contradictions. But I've seen it over and over: people say one thing on the podium and then go home and do the opposite. They're for freedom and justice in public, but at home they're the oppressor – the bourgeoisie.

Ryan, a young acquaintance behind bars whose picture-perfect upbringing in a "religious" family was only a façade, knows exactly what Shakur is talking about. A popular student at the private Catholic school he attended from first grade on, Ryan always had friends and enjoyed his reputation as class clown. A promising athlete, he played baseball, basketball, soccer, and hockey; a model Christian, he attended church and even became an altar boy. Yet his life was anything but happy:

> Everything in our home revolved around money and what "the neighbors" might think. And every-

thing looked good on the outside. Our family had achieved what most people deem "success." But behind the front door there were scenes of mental and emotional murder.

My father worked very hard at making his company successful, so I saw very little of him. He worked sixteen-hour days. My mother, on the other hand, was out of control – violent as a wild cat, and extremely selfish. She had a tongue like a bomb, but never used it to talk. She screamed. Even when she wasn't having a temper tantrum she was never warm, never said, "I love you," or "I'm sorry." She downright resented being a mother! And the words she used stung – they really stung: "You're just a guest in my house," she'd snarl. "Why don't you just get out of my hair. Go do something for your brain." By the time I was a teen I felt crushed and awkward and had no self-esteem or self-worth.

As far as religion went, we attended church as a family at Christmas and Easter (the rest of the time I went by myself), but the only time I heard my mother talk about God at home was to justify a rule or a punishment. There wasn't a bible in the house. Picture this: you send all your kids to a Catholic school, but you yourself don't even believe…

In high school I fell in with the "wrong" crowd and started to experiment with drugs and alcohol; I guess I did it to "fit in." Then I started stealing to support my habit. By the time I was eighteen I had attempted suicide and been arrested for assault with a weapon. I wound up in drug rehab. Later I joined the Navy, though I was kicked out after testing positive for cocaine...

Relationships? The only positive thing I can think of is that I never got a woman pregnant. But I've lied, cheated, and stole my way through my whole adult life. I've never paid a loan, never paid taxes, never held a bank account for more than six months. I've lived in cars, on park benches and stranger's couches, and in hospitals.

I'm very uncomfortable saying all this, because I have always hid behind a very favorable mask: my intellect, my charm, my good looks. God might still be able to love me, but I always worry that if people knew about my past, they'd run. And the last thing I need is the pain of rejection...

Nobody has a hard time accepting that evil exists like a plague. But at the same time everyone pretends it can be overcome with that old religious hocus-pocus: say your prayers, stay in school, and take your vitamins. Like that is all we need!

Cindi, a youth worker currently living in Boston, did not grow up in a religious home. Neither of her parents abused her. Still, the gulf between her father's promises of love and his abandonment of the family when she was five has left indelible scars. As in Ryan's case she knows that no matter the cause of a frayed family relationship, it often ends with a child who is sidelined to make room for other, more important adult priorities. And she also knows that sometimes it is impossible to lie to a child:

> They sat all four of us down on the couch. I was five. They used that word – divorce – and I had no idea what it meant, but I looked up and saw my older brother start bawling. Then I knew something was wrong so I started crying. We all went up to bed and Mom asked each one of us who we wanted to live with. Of course, we really didn't understand the question, but I remember, when she left for the boys' room, the fear that they were going to be divided from us girls. It was such a relief that they weren't.
>
> Later that night I went downstairs to get a glass of water. I saw Dad walking out with a suitcase in hand, and his alarm clock with the cord wrapped

around it. He looked at me and said "Honey, remember, Daddy loves you," and then he walked out. That memory is so vivid. He really did just walk out...

Today, as an adult, Cindi shows no sign of the brokenness that crushed her as a child and haunted her as a suicidal teen. Helping dozens of young women on a daily basis, she has turned her experience to a positive end; the same pain that once threatened to destroy her now enables her to offer guidance of a sort that adults with happy childhoods might never be able to give. But she still wonders at times about the meaning of love:

> What does it mean when a father tells his little girl, "I love you," but then walks out on you? It's even hard to trust that my husband really loves me...
>
> What I remember most as a child is this terrible void. I did everything I could to try and fill it. But because I couldn't fill it up with my father's love, I sought it elsewhere.
>
> I was fourteen when I lost my virginity. It was with an older guy I had started dating. It was like I was looking for someone to control me or to be above me. Later he became abusive, and my mom found out about it, so she ended it immediately.

The guy ended up stalking me for two years after that, but in a way I didn't mind: I actually fed off his attention. It made me feel like someone really cared about me.

In high school I was bulimic and battled other problems too. I hated being alone. Whenever I was, I'd just drink to a frenzy, and when I was drunk I would write and write in my journal. I always felt that my fears and insecurities had something to do with my father not being there. I cried and cried to him, and asked him why he couldn't just come home…Even now, it's like I'm still waiting for him to come home.

Statistically, separation and divorce have long been the most likely outcomes of marriage. But they are never the one-time legal incidents they appear. And that is why – no matter how "necessary" the divorce – it is always good to be reminded what it looks like through the eyes of a child, especially one who senses that it may define her, emotionally and psychologically, for the rest of her life.

Still, it is heartless (and useless) to condemn couples who divorce; as Anne, an English friend whose father left the house when she was a child, puts it, "Adults in crisis are desperate and do what they must." And though Anne concedes that children usually pay the brunt of the consequences, she notes that adults pay too. Further, she pleads that the pain caused by divorce must not be the end of every story:

> I had a very good mother, and even after she made the choice for divorce (the only option she saw), she was faithful to me. She sacrificed the joys of motherhood and worked full-time to support me, and her loyalty pulled me through. She gave me her best years – twenty-one of them.
>
> Yes, divorce always scars both partners, and if they have children, it scars them as well. But from my own life I know that my mother's decision to put my needs before hers saved me. It offered me the chance of recovery. I'm still "on the road," but I know full healing and wholeness will come.

Without women like Cindi and Anne – that is, without the resilience shown by every child who overcomes the obstacles of adult hypocrisies and failings – parenting would indeed be a bleak challenge. With them we can see that no matter how tempting it may be to despair over past mistakes, even the worst father or mother has a right to hope.

Addressing the question of parental shortcomings, and reminding us in a more general way of the source of that hope, Malcolm X once wrote:

> Children teach us a lesson adults should learn: to not be ashamed of failing, but to get up and try again. Most of us adults are so afraid, so cautious, so "safe" and therefore so shrinking and rigid... That it is why so many humans fail. Most middle-aged adults have resigned themselves to failure.

Of all the parents I know who have been tempted to give up, none has as much reason for resignation as Kareem, a "lifer" whose case I have followed for several years.

A native of Brooklyn who grew up in the city's worst projects, Kareem attended what was at the time the deadliest high school in the country in terms of homicides. His childhood ended when he was six, he says, the night he found his mother hanging from the ceiling of her bedroom. Later, as the father of a three-year-old who could already tell the difference between the sound of fire crackers, automobile back-fires, and gunshots, he decided to move to our semi-rural county. He was sick of the streets, and desperate to put an end to the cycle of crime and poverty that had plagued his family generation after generation.

When I first heard of Kareem, he was making headlines for the kidnapping, rape, and murder of a local eight-year-old. Kareem lived only a twenty-minute drive from my home, and in the months following his arrest, I visited him in the county prison. We have since stayed in touch, though he is now serving a life sentence without parole, hundreds of miles away.

Given the unspeakable evil of the crimes he admits having committed, Kareem may always feel burdened by his guilt, even though his remorse has given him some sense of peace. (In the last year, he has changed so completely that fellow inmates have begun calling him "Reverend" and turn to him for advice.) But aside from his guilt, he carries another, even heavier burden: the knowledge that he is not only a convicted murderer, but also a father whose failure has robbed him for good of the chance to bring up his children in the way he once dreamed.

But the story doesn't end there. Two years ago, Kareem's son entered the third grade in my church's parochial school; since then, he has blossomed socially, academically, and in every other way. Best of all, the boy's progress has given his father such hope that he has stopped torturing himself over his family's fate and started trying to make up for lost time – despite the fact that his fathering is limited to letters and rare visits, even though he knows that the deepest change of heart cannot release him from his bars.

Just weeks ago, as I began this book, Kareem Jr.'s teacher showed me a poem the boy had written about his father, which I would like to include here:

> My dad is the man. Do you understand?
> He gives me all the love he can...
> My dad wants me to learn in school:
> He thinks that learning is real cool.
> For my birthday he gave me a bike,
> He knew just what I would like.
> Every week he sends me mail.
> My love for dad will never fail...
> One day my dad and I will see
>   the Rocky Mountain snow.
> We'll find some gold,
>   more than we can ever hold.
> We'll take it home to mom:

"Look, mom, at this gold!"
We'll trade all this gold to get my dad home…
Even though I may not see my dad again,
My dad will always be my best friend.

It is said that dreamers, not realists, change the world. If that sounds like a threadbare cliché, it is only because we have made it one. Through their eyes of hope, children really do have power to transform reality. True, their naiveté may need to be eased away as they grow up, but we must never rob them of their optimism or dampen their joy. It is no small thing to affirm the importance of a child's longings. No matter how unrealistic they may seem to our adult minds, the world desperately needs their dreams.

6. The Easy Way Out

> There are two main human sins
> from which all others derive:
> impatience and indolence.
>
> FRANZ KAFKA

Ask anyone to name the chief dangers facing children today, and they're likely to tick off a predictable list – homelessness and malnutrition, poor education and inadequate healthcare. They're not wrong. But the longer I work with children, the more concerned I am about another quiet wave that carries just as a great a menace: the mindset of avoidance. Call it what you want – convenience, denial, or stubbornness – but if there's anything that characterizes education across the board, it's the persistent habit of turning our backs on the hardest questions, and falling for the answers that soothe us back to sleep.

Though the tendency to settle for the most painless solution to a problem is a normal human trait, it is rarely a healthy approach to child rearing. Of course, the very idea that parenting is a "problem" is a negative one. After all, raising the children we bring into the world ought to be a privilege and a joy. Yet fewer and fewer parents view their natural responsibilities in these positive terms. And the result is that fatherhood is no longer a natural duty, but one governments must chase men to fulfill; motherhood is at once attacked and seen as the supreme sacrifice; and loving (now downgraded to "bonding") is regarded as an art or a learnable skill.

From parenting journals to popular books, the wisdom is the same: children may be cute, but raising them is a thankless chore. That's why magazines are always advising couples to get away for romantic candlelight dinners, for vacations or long weekends by themselves. Just don't ask where the children fit into these plans: they rarely do – which is sad, because in actual fact, it's the hours you spend with your children when they are growing up that will later stand out as some of the happiest of your marriage. As for the struggles, sacrifices, and hard times, they are just as formative and important. Happy memories are just that – happy – but it's the rough patches that really strengthen relationships and temper the ties that bind.

Why is it that in bringing up our children, we so quickly see the obstacles and problems, and so easily miss the joys? Why are we so eager to protect ourselves from pain, and so reluctant to accept the hard work we know child-rearing must entail? Why are we so desperate to avoid the hard parts of parenting, and so blind to the ways they could help us to grow? Clare, a member of my church, says:

> Perhaps it's because our generation never really grew up. Many of us are still seeking the perfect partner, the perfect car, or some other kind of elusive happiness. We don't know what it is to make sacrifices, to give unselfishly in ways that won't ever be recognized. I'm not sure we were ever expected to...

Clearly not everyone is in the same boat. Plenty of parents feel like Jane, another member of my church (and mother of five), who says:

> I think motherhood is the noblest task of all, because you cannot do it at your convenience, or tailor it to suit your preferences. You have to be ready to give up everything when you take on this task: your time, restful nights, your hobbies, your pursuit of physical fitness, any beauty you may have had, and all of the private little pleasures you might have counted as a right, from late dinners and long soaks in the tub to weekend excursions and cycling trips…I'm not saying you can't have any of these things, but you have to be ready to let them all go if you're going to have children and put them first.

To many women, especially in underdeveloped nations, the idea of giving up these things would hardly seem a sacrifice. They are trappings of a comfortable life, ones that only people with a high standard of living can attain. And even if our own wealth allows us to take them for granted, it never hurts to be reminded of that. Neither should we forget that in relieving us of almost every task our grandparents once performed – from cutting wood and plowing to building fires and carrying water – technological progress has shielded us not only from the discomfort of sweaty labor and long waits, but also the formation of character it yields. Because we are no longer familiar with the meaning of hardship, we can no longer pass on its value to our children.

Where I grew up, hard physical work was part of daily life. One did not need to look for it. There was no indoor plumbing, no central heating, and, for many years, no electricity. Meals were cooked on an open fire, and there was always wood to split and stack, and water to carry. Grass was cut with a machete; it was coarse, heavy, and high, especially after rainfall. As a teenager especially, I grumbled incessantly about the never-ending chores, but my parents had no pity. And in retrospect I am grateful. I see now how their insistence taught me self-discipline, concentration, perseverance, and the ability to carry through – all things you need to be a father.

Few parents I know carry water anymore, but they're fooling themselves if they think raising a child doesn't involve hard work. Take discipline, for instance. To hold out firmly and consistently against a child's will is often irksome. It is always easier to let things slide. Yet anyone who prizes comfort above the effort of demanding obedience will find that, in the long run, the problem will grow bigger and bigger.

German educator Friedrich Wilhelm Foerster, a friend of my grandparents, used to tell of a British general who walked his horse through a street corner again and again, until the stubborn mare turned the way he had taught it to. "Never give in till the battle is won," he said after the nineteenth time, as the animal finally turned as he wished. Exasperating as the incident must have been, the lesson it contains is a vital one for every parent.

Sometimes we skirt a difficult issue simply because we feel too weary to confront it. At other times our reluctance is connected to guilt: Why be hard on your children when you've made the same mistakes? Then there are the times we are blinded by pity, when we try to smooth things over to avoid causing hurt. Such thinking rarely has immediate consequences, so we forget them, ignore them, or talk them away. But there will always be repercussions, and they can sometimes be ugly. Bea, an acquaintance, has a classic example:

> I had a friend, Kate, who tried to commit suicide three times in high school. Her family always rushed her to the emergency room, and had her stomach pumped (she took pills each time), and she'd soon be back at school. They never really helped her...Kate's parents had divorced some years before, and then remarried, and neither set of parents really wanted her. She was a constant reminder to them of their pasts, and they wanted to get on with their lives. She didn't fit into their plans.

Paul, another acquaintance, suffered similar anguish. Born out of wedlock, he grew up without a father, and while his mother tried to protect him by avoiding the subject, her silence ended up making his life hell.

> I grew up with my mother in the Midwest. "Hometown America." I sometimes asked about my father. Mom would show me a photograph and tell me he was smart and handsome and daring, and that he wanted to be with us, but that other people needed him more than we did. I

never asked too many questions. Maybe I could feel that it was hard for her to talk about it. But over the years I guess I built up this picture of my father, the cartoon hero – a daring man who was always off on some mission, rescuing people in distress.

When I was fourteen, I discovered by chance who my father was and where he lived. I also found out that he had been married for nearly forty years, though not to my mother. It's strange to realize it now, but I'm not sure the thought ever even crossed my mind that my father could be someone else's father as well, or that I might be "illegitimate." If it did, I certainly never faced up to it...I never talked with my mother about my feelings; I just let them fester. Soon my fantasy father evolved into a villain. I hated him. I began to resent anybody being nice to me – I knew they were just having pity on the little charity case, the little bastard...

I ran away from home, I was so determined to prove myself without help from anybody. But I ended up just running from place to place. I got involved in drugs and only avoided jail when a friend bailed me out...There were other tight spots I weaseled out of, but mostly I ran when the going got tough; I just couldn't face up to my own mistakes. Once I was doped up and missed work and was so ashamed that I just skipped town. I never even went back to face the boss. I was constantly on the run, because I was always messing up and there was no way I could hang around and try to straighten things up.

Everywhere I went I was attracted to homosexual pick-up spots. I wasn't looking for relationships, just anonymous sex, and if anything started getting serious, I got out in a hurry.

After a few years of that, I settled down somewhat. I went to school, then grad school, got married, and became an upright citizen. But it was all just show. I was still trying to run away from my past, just like my parents had...It didn't work. My wife thought I was clean, but I was still sneaking off to sex shops and doing drugs on the sly.

Through it all I wanted so bad to be loved, though I never dared give anybody a chance to really get to know me...

Both Kate and Paul's stories show that it makes no difference why we push down a problem or look the other way. In the one case, the issue was lovelessness; in the other, a mother's understandable desire to protect her son from shame. As for the results, they were basically the same: confrontations were avoided, but not pain. If anything, that was only compounded.

Even when we do face a challenge that comes our way, we often fail to meet it squarely. And while there's nothing wrong with an easy answer in itself, the quick fix is rarely the best one. In fact, the hard truth is that the most convenient solution may hide the gravest dangers. But in a land of fast food and credit cards, tanning salons and 24-hour TV, that's not popular advice.

No one can deny that five minutes at a drive-through can replace an hour at the kitchen, but neither can we claim innocence with regard to the skyrocketing rates of obesity among children on both sides of the Atlantic. Nor should those of us whose TV doubles as entertainer and unpaid nanny be surprised that our children are addicted to the mindless junk it spews, that they find reading a drag, and that they insist on our buying them the latest brands. (My children were brought up in a TV-less house, and they have all continued the tradition in their own homes.)

And while circumstances like ignorance or poverty are often used to rationalize the bad choices parents make – with regard to nutrition, for instance – the fact is that even the best explanation cannot save a child from the consequences. In any case, the problem is never a purely financial one: well-educated, wealthy parents are just as negligent as less privileged ones.

According to Jennifer, a teacher at an upscale Los Angeles day care center, even salaried professionals are too harried to attend to their children's most basic needs:

> Since most of my kids come from middle-class and upper middle-class homes, you'd never think they'd arrive without having had breakfast. But it happens all the time. They come to day care flat-out hungry.
>
> I had one three-year-old who was given a little chocolate for breakfast and some more chocolate for lunch. That was it! And her mother is an executive who makes good money. The girl had a protruding stomach and no energy whatsoever...
>
> I spoke to her parents, but nothing changed. Now the girl's been diagnosed with a sugar disorder

and continues to suffer the effects, including leth-
argy, bloating, and circles under her eyes. She has
very little desire to learn, and constantly wants to
be cuddled. It breaks my heart...

I hear more and more mothers say, "I can't wait
till Monday." It seems that being with their own
children for an "entire" weekend is all they feel
they can take. They've definitely chosen their
lifestyle, and they are determined to keep it. But
the children don't feel wanted. They are angry and
frustrated, and if you ask me, it's all because they've
been made to feel guilty for wanting to spend time
with their parents.

Childhood itself has come to be viewed as a suspect
phase. Never mind toddlers who are made to feel
guilty. On top of that, children of all ages and means
are being squelched on the playground and in class,
not because they're unmanageable or unruly, but
simply because they're behaving like children should.
Diagnosed with "problems" that used to be recognized as normal childhood traits – impulsiveness and
exuberance, spontaneity and daring – millions of children are being diagnosed as hyperactive and drugged
into submission. I'm referring, of course, to the widespread use of Ritalin and other related stimulants, and

to the public's fascination with medicine as the answer to any and every problem.

Ritalin is surely a legitimate drug for certain specific conditions. But given the threefold increase in its use in the last decade, one has to wonder if it isn't being misused as an easy cure-all for problems such as ADHD (attention deficit-hyperactivity disorder) and to rein in lively children who may not even have the disorder. After all, much of what is designated as ADHD is nothing more than a defense against over-structuring – a natural reflex that used to be called letting off steam – or alternately, a symptom of various unmet emotional needs. Jeff, an old friend, gives a poignant example:

> Jerome, an eight-year-old from Seattle, came and stayed with us last summer for a break from the city. When he arrived he was a mess, though he was on Ritalin. After two or three days, however, we weaned him off his dose, because with all the room to play he was no longer bouncing off the walls, but beginning to take himself in hand. (At home in his apartment building there was nothing for him to do but watch TV.) I could definitely see the change.

When this little guy first arrived he could barely keep his attention on anything for more than a minute, he was so keyed up and distracted. I laid down some ground rules and gave him some time. I took him out with a bike, since he was unsure of how to ride...By the end of his stay he was so settled and happy that at one point he even asked me if he could call me Dad. I just about lost it. This child didn't need Ritalin: all he needed was fresh air – and love.

Put Jerome back in the projects, and he will probably revert. He'll be put back on Ritalin, and his "symptoms" will be re-suppressed. Whether he'll ever get the attention he really needs, either at home or at school, is quite another question. Fortunately it's one that increasing numbers of people are asking, like Peter Breggin, a pediatrician and author best known for his book *Talking Back to Ritalin:*

> People call drugs like Ritalin a godsend for emotional and behavioral problems...But I think the way they're overused is absolutely horrifying. When I was asked by the National Institutes of Health to be a scientific discussant on the effects of these drugs at a conference they held, I reviewed the important literature, and I found that when

animals are given them, they stop playing; they stop being curious; they stop socializing; they stop trying to escape. Ritalin makes good caged animals...We're making good caged kids. It's all very well to talk about it taking a whole village to raise a child, but in practice, we're acting as if we think it only takes a pill.

As if this medical suppression of childhood (Breggin calls it "chemical straitjacketing") were not enough, there are myriad other ways in which children fall prey to our addiction to convenience and control. Most shocking of all is the great number of abuses committed against children, not by strangers and not even by recognized criminals, but simply by their own parents and caregivers – "normal" people who snap because things don't go the way they want them to.

Equally chilling is the number of abortions had by women who terminate pregnancies not because they do not want children, but because pregnancy interferes with other plans. According to a 1996 article in the *British Medical Journal,* attitudes in some parts of Europe (and the United States is surely no different) are such that some women choose to abort simply because their baby's due date conflicts with a planned vacation.

Unbelievable as such a mindset sounds, it is not entirely inexplicable. As Foerster points out in his classic *Basics of Education,* the comforts of contemporary "civilization" have cushioned life so completely that many people simply do not have the wherewithal to deal with anything that makes demands on them. Faced with the simple unpredictability of life – not to mention pain, suffering, hard work, or sacrifice – they helplessly succumb "as if to hard blows…They do not know what to make of frustration – how to make something constructive of it – and see it only as something that oppresses and irritates." And though, he goes on, these very things provided earlier generations with the experiences through which they gained mastery over life's challenges, they are often "enough to send the rootless, modern person into a mental institution." Or, as we have seen, to prisons and abortion clinics.

Given the dismal state of the culture described above, parenting in the 21st century is clearly going to involve a lot of hard work. But why should that frighten us? As long as we run from the responsibilities that will always be there, we will not only squander the most formative moments of bringing up children, but rob ourselves as well of its most meaningful joys. And if that sounds like a stretch of the imagination, listen to Chuck, a California acquaintance for whom the easy solution to just about everything disappeared when a plane crash left him paralyzed from the waist down:

> Despite the accident I was fortunate enough to get into law school...and after I finished, my wife Karen and I moved to North Carolina, to be near my parents. We knew we could never have a family of our own. Then Karen, who has always had a heart for kids at risk, discovered that our county had a serious need for foster parents, and after some investigation we realized that we could raise a family, after all. We decided to start with a couple of children...We now have the two we started with, plus three others, all of whom we've adopted, and two more whom we hope to adopt as well.
>
> We are always amazed at how people respond to our situation. Forget my disability – even without that, people think we are crazy. But we would rather be seen as eccentric and have children than

be what society calls normal…In actual fact, it's the reactions we get that don't make sense. On the one hand, everyone recognizes how hostile the world has become for children. On the other, very few are willing to change their lifestyles in order to fit children into their lives. We are so quick to point the finger at everyone but ourselves.

People are always complaining about how bad things are and how difficult their children are. But how often is this because they are too busy, too driven, and too selfish? How often is it just because they won't let themselves be inconvenienced? Disciplining and training and nurturing a child is inconvenient. But it is also the most redemptive thing…Sure, there are days when your buttons get pushed, times when you are at your wits' end – but a little child can put everything back in perspective.

In my view, bringing up children is the best venture there is, even if the fruits will only be harvested in the next generation. How fulfilling is that? I'd prefer to let people answer that for themselves.

7. In Praise of Black Sheep

I am convinced that there is ten times
more good than bad in a child,
and about the bad, we can wait and see.

JANUSZ KORCZAK

In a culture teeming with hyper-competitive
parents – and myriad opportunities to compete – it's
easy enough to find teen pop queens and academic
whiz kids, precocious computer scientists and pint-
sized tennis stars. These days, the models that smile
from glossy magazines are often high school girls;
and teenage businessmen make headlines buying and
selling stocks on the Internet.

As with every trend, however, there's another side that doesn't make the news, and stories that won't make you smile. It's the worrying statistics on high school dropouts and teen suicides, "underachievers" and children behind bars. It's the quiet pain of the obese, the awkward, the disabled, and the slow. It's the epidemic of the hyperactive, the addicted, the medicated, and the depressed. And at the bottom of everyone's list, it's the scarred childhoods of those who lack warmth, hope, and encouragement, not because there's anything wrong with them, but simply because they've been made to feel that they're losers.

There's a black sheep in every flock, or so the saying goes, and because it is so true, there are few of us who don't know one, or didn't know one as a child. Every family, every class, has one: that brother or sister, boy or girl, who's always in trouble, who's prone to stretch limits or take things "too far," who's embarrassingly honest, who never fits in. It's that child over whom every teacher puzzles longest and every parent loses the most sleep.

But no matter how natural the phenomenon, being a misfit is never easy. At least that's what Dana, a woman who suffered finger-pointing and rejection for years, says:

> Even as a very young child I always told people exactly what I thought, though this was seldom appreciated. If someone had a blemish on their face, or their stockings didn't match their dress, if they hobbled or snuffled or had a nervous twitch, I always pointed it out. If I would see an adult who looked depressed, I would ask them what was wrong. And of course I was always reprimanded...
>
> I'm grateful that much of my childhood is a blur now, but I can never forget the feeling of being the black sheep – always in trouble, and always accused of creating trouble.
>
> In school, an exclusive private one, I stole, cheated, and lied. I stuck to myself a lot, and when I felt picked on I could be mean. But I was also very insecure. It didn't help that I was labeled early on, especially by a particular teacher, as the one to watch out for. That reputation followed me wherever I went, and helped people assume that I was always about to act out. The subs at school were all advised, "Watch out for her, that's why she's in the front row." I was also singled out constantly for punishments that no one else in my

class seemed bad enough to merit. I lied to keep out of trouble, then got caught and lied more.

Before long every teacher at school seemed to know how bad I was, and soon even my classmates began to treat me differently. Luckily there was Louisa, a girl with Down syndrome, who liked me as I was, talked with me, and treated me with respect; I will never forget her.

As for my own parents, they were frustrated by all the bad reports, and usually sided with the school. After all, they had worked hard to enroll me there. I don't ever remember any hugs or other expressions of companionship in those years. There was only one long, angry talk after another.

By the time I left elementary school, I had given up on myself. And why not? No one else seemed to believe in me. Though frustrated, I steeled myself against every emotion and became a walking stone. I couldn't cry for years. At the same time I suffered constant nervous indigestion and diarrhea. I was an emotional wreck.

Looking back on my childhood now, I'm sure I was not without guilt. I probably was a difficult child in many respects. But should a kid ever feel given up on, or marked to the point where she despairs? Isn't it the right of every child to feel that at least someone believes in her, and that things can indeed change? I'm still hopeful of that for myself, though I am not entirely sure. Not long ago I bumped into an old classmate who seemed ashamed of seeing me again. When I asked her why, she looked embarrassed but then confided that after all these years she still remembered her mother's warnings about me.

While the tribulations of a woman like Dana may seem negligible compared to physical and sexual abuse, they are not. As her story shows, the weight of a negative label can be just as impossible for a child to carry. In any case, the emotional suffering of a child is never insignificant. Because they are so vulnerable, and because they are dependent on the adults around them, children are, in my experience, far more sensitive to criticism than one might guess, and far more easily crushed. And even if their natural forgetfulness and their amazing capacity to forgive relieves most children of much that might burden an adult, there are those whose self-confidence can be shriveled by an unjust accusation, a cutting remark, or a hasty miscalculation.

Even when we don't label a child, we may subconsciously categorize him, which can be equally harmful, because it influences the way we treat him. We do this more often than we might realize, sometimes even without knowing a thing about the child in question. Gary, an old friend in England who recently took his class on a field trip to Northern Ireland, recalls:

> It happened in Belfast. I was outside our bus trying to keep the local boys and girls away from the vehicle, but to no avail. Those kids were so excited we had stopped in their street that they just swarmed all over it. Finally I got upset and chased them away. Just then a woman on the sidewalk came over. She apologized for the way the children had clamored to get on board, and said she understood why I felt I had to shoo them away. But then she began to tell me about the kids: "Those two boys over there, they're five and eight. Their father just hanged himself two weeks ago. That one there never had a father; and this little boy over here – his father's been in prison for years. No one takes much notice of them." It hit me right in the stomach. Here I was, writing off a bunch of street urchins and treating them as troublemakers, and they were actually victims of the worst neglect...

Whenever we pass judgment on a child, we fail to see him as a whole person. True, he may be nervous, shy, stubborn, moody, or violent; we may know his siblings or his background, or think we recognize family traits. But to focus on any one aspect of a child, especially a negative one, is to put him in a box whose sides may not really be determined by reality, but only by our own expectations. And to categorize him as a result is to forget that his destiny was not placed in our hands. It may also limit his potential and thus the person he will become.

Comparing children – whether our own or other people's – is just as bad as labeling them. Obviously, every child is different. Some seem to get all the lucky breaks, while others have a rough time simply coping with life. One child consistently brings home perfect scores, while the next is always at the bottom of the class. Another is gifted and popular, while still another, no matter how hard he tries, is always in trouble and often gets forgotten. Children must be brought up to accept these facts. But as parents, we must do our part, too, and refrain from showing favoritism, and from comparing our children with others. Above all, we must refrain from pushing them to become something that their unique personal makeup may never allow them to be.

A child's abilities should never be stifled or ignored. Yet there are dangers in actively encouraging them. It is no small task to guide a child who has been made overly conscious of her talents, and when this is the result of flattery, it is even harder. Add to that an exaggerated notion of self-worth, which is almost always acquired at the expense of others, and you have a child who may have great difficulty relating to her peers.

It is the same with the extra attention and subtle favoritism given to children whose physical attractiveness, sunny smiles, and easy-going personalities allow them to glide through childhood. As my grandfather used to put it, such children are saddled with a "golden curse" – the dangerous illusion that because everything and everyone favored them in childhood, the adult world will treat them the same way.

Louise, an elderly neighbor and retired teacher, knows all about the harm that can be done to children in this way:

Flattery has had a devastating influence in my life. When I was five or six, I remember going out with my sisters, my mother, and two aunts for a Sunday afternoon walk. We children ran happily ahead, but I was soon holding back to catch the conversation. I had heard my name. As I listened, I swelled with pride: they were talking about my talents and gifts, and one of them called me "that wonderful child."

I could never forget this conversation! The damage was done. Now I had an image of myself, and I had to work to keep it up, even when my life began to fall apart. I couldn't be myself, but instead became ambitious, dishonest, and twisted. Looking back on it I see from that point on, I was no longer a real child...

Korczak points out that we must be careful not to equate difficult children with "bad" ones, and thus stifle "the things that temper their spirit, that make up the driving force behind their demands and intentions, and constitute their will and their freedom." He similarly warns against confusing "good" children with merely "easy" ones:

The good child cries very little, he sleeps through the night, he is confident and good-natured. He is well-behaved, convenient, obedient, and good. Yet no consideration is given to the fact that he may grow up to be indolent and stagnant.

Neither should we forget that raising a "good" child is a dubious goal in the first place, if only because the line between instilling integrity and breeding self-righteousness is so fine. As educator Thomas Lickona has pointed out, getting into trouble can be a vital part of building a child's character:

> You want to encourage obedience, but you don't want to stifle independence. It's wisely been said that every child should have the confidence to mis-behave occasionally. Giving kids room to be less than perfect is important…The girl who's a "little angel" as a child isn't necessarily the one who'll make a resourceful, independent adult.

While excessive praise can harm a "good" child, the negative comparisons that leave another one feeling that he is "bad" can be downright devastating. That is because as long as we compare the "bad" child's qualities to those of the "good" one, we tie his self-esteem to his ability to keep up with someone else, and thus trap him in a cycle of endless frustration. In the worst cases, such treatment can lead to emotional breakdown, as happened in the following case, which Fran, an acquaintance who used to work in a large psychiatric clinic, recently related to me:

> One day I was called in to see Michael, an eleven-year-old, in the ward for children with profound multiple disabilities. Diagnosed with acute autism, Michael had always fluctuated between complete withdrawal and violent outbursts. But now the violence seemed to be increasing and the staff wondered if there was any pattern in the change.
>
> As normal procedure, I spent a number of sessions simply observing Michael and his routine, making exact notes of activities, reactions, etc. It was a remarkable case, because we did not often see such clear patterns of stimulus and response, even in less profoundly disabled children. It was all the more surprising to find it in a child classified as being completely out of touch with the world around him. In certain circumstances, Michael was clearly capable of communication, logical thought, and controlled responses.
>
> At first, I was cautious in sharing my observations with the staff. No one would have believed that a child with "normal" learning abilities could ever have been admitted to that ward in the first place. Instead, we initiated several months of thorough diagnostic work, including a visit to Michael's

family. That home visit will always remain one of my worst memories.

Michael's father, a pharmacist, was extremely proud of Michael's older brother, who had been a model child with accelerated development. When Michael lagged in speech development – compared to the older brother – the father had immediately arranged for speech therapy. The same pattern continued over the years: continual measuring and comparing with the older brother and intense therapy in a desperate effort to bring Michael up to the expected level. Michael rebelled more and more against these expectations and the therapy, closing up in himself. His violent outbursts were undoubtedly a mechanism for defending his right to be who he was – not signs of aggression. But one violent weekend, the parents called for medical help because they couldn't handle it anymore. Michael was brought into the clinic as an eight-year-old and he never left it again.

It is tragic, but nothing could convince Michael's parents that there was genuine hope for his condition. Even during our conversation, they constantly compared him with his brother. They were no longer capable of seeing Michael for himself. I had to resign myself to the fact that Michael would never return home. The best we could do was to arrange for him to be transferred into another section of the clinic where he would receive therapy and attention.

I often wonder now how many children with emotional problems are simply showing a healthy reaction against the pressures put on them by their parents...

Though the number of children abused in such a terrible way is surely small, Michael's story still serves as a vital warning to every parent: your children are not your property, and any attempt to make them "perform" or measure up will sooner or later end in their destruction. Even if the outcome is less dramatic, the sapping of a child's self-confidence is always a serious thing; to my mind, it is no different from what the Germans call *Seelenmord* – soul murder.

Constant pressure of any kind will eventually cause a child to snap – and when it happens, the end result may not only be emotional but also physical violence. One need only look at the wave of school and high school shootings that have swept the United States in recent years: in one case, the gunman (really a child) had been hounded by his mother because of his weight; in two others, the shooters felt constantly compared to a popular, athletic sibling. And even if such roots of distress cannot explain or justify a terrible crime, they are still part of the picture, and thus ought never be ignored.

Thankfully, most mothers and fathers know when they've pushed a child too far – like the couple whose story follows:

> When we first looked into adopting Sandy, a three-year-old with fetal alcohol syndrome who is now a grown woman living on her own, we were warned that she was not "normal." From the moment we met her, however, we were quite sure that the doctors were wrong. It was true that she was developmentally delayed in her speech, but that could be corrected. Or so we thought.
>
> Within months of Sandy's joining our family we enrolled her in an individual speech therapy program at a local university but very soon realized it was not what she needed. She was completely uncooperative; something in her rebelled against our attempts to "help" her develop. We pulled her out, and wondered what we should try next...

By the time she was ready for first grade Sandy had learned to talk, but her vocabulary was very limited, and she was often frustrated that she could not express herself. By then we were somewhat resigned to the fact that she had a real learning disability. We gave her special tutoring and other one-to-one help, but the more attention she got, the more frustrated she became.

As Sandy got older we tried to encourage her by telling her that "everyone is different," and that there were many things that she could do better than other children her age. Yes, many things, but not school work! With all our efforts, she had gotten the clear message that academic performance was the most important thing.

With adolescence the problems only escalated. Eighth grade special ed totally backfired. As far as Sandy was concerned, it might as well have been emblazoned in neon above the classroom door: "You kids are failures!" For her, the whole idea of separate classes added insult to the injuries she already suffered; it was like salt in an open wound. She became increasingly unhappy, depressed, and self-conscious. The pressures – subtle ones from us as parents, and real ones from peers – nearly drove her crazy.

When Sandy was fifteen, we finally decided to take her out of school altogether. (It was then, ironically, without any social or academic pressures, that she began to read – for enjoyment.) But her problems were far from over. Well-meaning adults would often ask her what she was learning, why she wasn't going to classes, or when she was planning to finish school. From every angle it seemed that she was still being hit over the head because of her academic failings.

Looking back to those years we can see that we were brainwashed, trapped into thinking that a conventional education means everything. Sandy just couldn't fit the mold. How could we have been so blind? Right from the very beginning we had tried much too hard to correct her expressions, to make her speech more intelligible, more socially acceptable instead of just listening to her and receiving her jumbled thoughts however they came out. The very idea of verbal development was not important to her, only to us.

We see now that, much as we loved our daughter, we did not truly accept her as she was – how God had made her. If only we could do it over again! We can't. But if we could we would be much less concerned about her inabilities (or our labels for those things) and more affirming of who she was – because there were plenty of things to affirm. Sandy had a great feeling for the underdog, the hurting, and the despised, and as a volunteer at L'Arche, an organization that cares for the mentally disabled, she demonstrated that even if she wasn't a scholar, she was a caring, capable adult...

Challenging as it is to raise a child with a special need such as fetal alcohol syndrome, it can be just as hard to bring up one who is merely difficult. With a disabled child there are specific issues to address. But what about the child whose disorder no one can diagnose? Sharon, the mother of a troubled young man in my neighborhood, recently wrote to me:

I sometimes think it might be easier to parent a physically disabled child than one who has an emotional disorder. When people have an obvious physical hindrance, you can at least see their difficulty, and their need for additional sensitivity and understanding...When a kid looks "normal," people often have trouble accepting the fact that he may have a hidden problem. To them, there's no reason why he shouldn't be expected to do as well as his peers.

Sharon has a point. Yet in my experience, the worst thing about the difficulties faced by children like her son is not that they are ignored by others, but that – as the following anecdote from a father in my church shows – they are often magnified by parents:

> Our eldest son James started out as a contented, undemanding child, until he was three. That was when we followed my job to another state, and he suddenly fell apart. At first he went back to square one on toilet training. Then, though he could still be his former sunny self, he started acting hyper a lot of the time, racing around the house – sometimes silently, his arms flailing like windmill blades, and sometimes shrieking with unbelievable energy. He also developed several nervous habits, including thumb-sucking and twisting and tugging his hair so constantly that a small bald spot developed and remained on top of his head…
>
> As James grew he became more and more antisocial, disrupting family gatherings and school and neighborhood events. He hated organized activities such as games, running away and lashing out at anyone who tried to encourage him to join in. He rebelled, loudly, at any hint of pressure to hurry with dressing or eating.

But why was he acting like this? What was wrong? We tried everything, from gentle talks to a spank on the bottom to time out (he loved time out). But nothing worked. No matter how we tried to get through to him, we couldn't seem to penetrate his little world, and even after the biggest blow-ups he seemed to emerge victorious...

James was never a tough or unfeeling child. One of his best friends was Sonia, a severely disabled woman who was wheelchair bound. Sonia was unable to speak and could neither feed nor dress herself – she really couldn't do anything other than smile, gurgle, and groan. But James loved being with her, even if it just meant holding her hand. (When asked why, he told her caregiver, "I don't know...She can love with her eyes, and you can feel it that she loves you!")

When he wasn't with Sonia, however, there were constant problems. Around us we saw parents who seemed so much more relaxed than we – people who appeared to be coping just fine, whose children seemed to respond to every piece of advice. Why didn't James? We questioned our parenting skills, blamed ourselves, and looked for deep-seated problems and hidden keys. We looked in the distant past and the murky depths. We looked at every possible cause of his apparent insecurities, in each other and in ourselves. And we went into tailspins...

When James was about eight, we moved again, and again his struggles intensified. Even the positive sides of his personality began to change for the worse. Once brimming with ideas, his creativity now disappeared. He stopped reading and doing projects; he lost his ability to concentrate enough to occupy himself; his bedwetting returned. Most disturbing of all, he became so violent and unpredictable that we could no longer trust him with his siblings.

Sometimes the smallest thing would set him off, and he would lose control completely, racing up and down the hall shouting "No! No! No!" slamming doors, and screaming at the objects and people in his way.

Through it all, our self-confidence slipped lower and lower. We talked, prayed, read, and talked more. We went to medical professionals and pediatric experts and parent-teacher conferences. We sought their advice and got it by the barrel full. But we didn't trust ourselves. Or James.

It was this, we realized in hindsight, that was our biggest problem: we had stopped acting on our own convictions and were looking for advice from others. Part of it was an exaggerated worry that James wouldn't "turn out right," which made us put him and ourselves under pressure to conform. Part of it was a feeling that his "failure" reflected badly on us, and the resulting fear – even if it was only subconsciously there – that he was a threat to our reputation. And part of it was the fact that, though we never entirely stopped hoping for it, we had given up believing in the possibility of change.

Thankfully, we had friends who continued to believe for us, and through their help we were eventually able to turn a corner and pull through. For me, the moment of truth came when I began to see that it was not James who was the cause of our troubles, or even myself, but simply my attitude toward the challenge of raising a child who didn't fit into the prescribed mold. Why should he fit in, anyway? Once I got that straight, things began to slide into place. First, I was able to give up my ideas of what James should be like, which made for fewer reasons to nag at him; second, there were fewer occasions for frustration, and so on...

In the last two years James has become more stable and happy than my wife and I have ever seen him. More important, we've changed. We are learning to be there for him, without agendas and without worries. As for the identification of his behavioral "condition" (something that still eludes us), we have come to recognize that even the most accurate diagnosis is useless without a cure. And the best cure is always love.

We'll never be a model family. But at least we're a stronger one. And if there's anything James has taught us, it's that the strongest family is the one in which each member knows he needs the others.

Given the intensity of a struggle like James's, it is often hard for parents to see the benefits of having raised a difficult child – even when the outcome is positive. For some, the heartache has simply taken too big a toll; for others, the sense of relief is so great that, once the battle is over, neither parent nor child ever choose to mention it again. But strange as it may sound, I believe that the more challenging the child, the more grateful the parent should be. If anything, parents of difficult children ought to be envied, because it is they, more than any others, who are forced to learn the most wonderful secret of true parenthood: the meaning of unconditional love. It is a secret that remains hidden from those whose love is never tested.

When we welcome the prospect of raising the problematic child with these things in mind, we will begin to see our frustrations as moments that can awaken our best qualities. And instead of envying the ease with which our neighbors seem to raise perfect offspring, we will remember that rule-breakers and children who show their horns often make more self-reliant and independent adults than those whose limits are never tried. In the words of Henry Ward Beecher, the progressive 19th-century preacher: "That energy that makes a child hard to manage is the energy that afterwards makes him a manager of life." And even if the trials of our own childhood leave us hesitant to embrace such a positive view, we can always look away from ourselves and to our children. In loving and being loved by them we will always rediscover the power of forgiving, the importance of leaving the past behind, and the optimism born of hope. To go back to Dana, the mother whose story opened this chapter:

> Wouldn't you know it – when my first son, Brian, started kindergarten, he was soon showing the same troublesome character I had as a child, and since then he's had problems with one teacher after

another. It's been a daily battle to make him behave, because I'm determined that none of my children will go through what I did...

Thanks to a wise teacher who refuses to dwell on his problems, however, I've learned to stop projecting my fears on him, to concentrate on his strengths, and to make sure that no one tries to take away my joy in him.

If Brian's like me, he will always be impulsive. As it is, he disobeys me every day, and I'm always having to make him feel the consequences. But I know that what my son needs most is not just discipline, but extra time and companionship. No matter what happens, he needs to know that as his mother I will always believe in him.

At a conference in the sixties, at a time when "maladjustment" was the educational catchphrase of the day, Martin Luther King shocked teachers and parents by turning the supposed problem on its head. "Thank God for maladjusted children," a colleague remembers him saying. More than just a sentimental defense on behalf of "difficult" (and underprivileged) children, King's attitude captures like nothing else the essence of what parenting is all about.

Instead of hushing up the children who embarrass us, instead of clamping down on the ones who don't fit in, instead of analyzing the troubled ones and drawing conclusions about their delinquent futures, we ought to welcome them all as they are. By helping us to discover the limitations of "goodness" and the boredom of conformity, they can teach us the necessity of genuineness, the wisdom of humility, and finally the reality that, in parenting as with anything else, nothing good is won without struggle.

8. Discovering Reverence

When a child walks down the road,
a company of angels goes before him
proclaiming, "Make way for
the image of the Holy One."

HASIDIC SAYING

In a society beset by countless problems, the greatest dangers to children seem obvious enough: poverty, violence, neglect, disease, abuse, and countless other ills. Visible or invisible, suffered or only seen, these evils have always been there, and everyone agrees that they are terrible things. But what can any one of us do to overcome them? In a 1919 essay on the question of social renewal, Hermann Hesse suggests that the first step is to recognize its root cause: our lack of reverence for life.

> All disrespect, all irreverence, all hard heartedness, all contempt is nothing else than killing. And it is possible to kill not only what is in the present, but also that which is in the future. With just a little witty skepticism we can kill a good deal of the future in a child or young person. Life is waiting everywhere, flowering everywhere, but we only see a small part of it and trample much of it with our feet...

In identifying irreverence as a power that kills life, Hesse touches on something that endangers children more than anything else in the world today. Irreverence for children pervades almost everything in our culture, including our speech. It is there in the flippant way in which we refer to them as "stinkers" and "little devils," in the sarcasm that allows us to laugh at their expense, in the disdain we have for their feelings when we discuss their shortcomings in front of them (or behind their backs). It is there, too, in our habit of categorizing them: in the way we gloat over one child and sigh over the next – even in the way we

unthinkingly call out-of-wedlock children "illegitimate." And words are the least of it.

As the chief symptom of lovelessness, irreverence
is a significant cause of every social ill mentioned in
this book – and if that sounds like an exaggeration,
one need only look at a widespread ill such as divorce for confirmation. With reverence, the mindset
that makes it "acceptable" would never be tolerated.
Ari, a friend at Columbia University, writes:

> To my mind, divorce is a deplorable breach of con-
> tract, and I say without humor that children should
> be allowed to sue. Consider the facts: Two people
> agree to create a human being and promise to give
> it love, a home, security, and happiness. They take
> this step with the best of intentions, to be sure, but
> then something goes awry. They find they really
> hate each other or for some other reason cannot
> live together. But in separating, they put them-
> selves first and forget about the contract they have
> with their child. I do not believe, as you often hear
> soon-to-be-divorced parents say, that the separa-
> tion will be "best for the child." My experience has
> taught me better.
>
> But didn't my parents spare me an unhappy
> home where fighting and angry confrontation

were the mode of communication? I believe not. I believe that they – as incompatible as they were and remain today – could have learned to stop shouting or slamming doors. At least they could have learned all that more easily than I learned to be a child of divorce.

With divorce so common these days, mine is not a popular position. Some – usually divorced people with children – accuse me of being selfish. But it's not just me. Someday they will hear it from their own children. A lost childhood cannot be recaptured.

Harsh as it seems, Ari's proposal is mild compared to what Jesus suggests for those who rob children of their childhood: "If anyone causes one of these to stumble, it would be better for him to be weighted with a millstone and cast into the sea." Even these words are understandable, however, in light of the spirit of reverence – the spirit that welcomes children and opposes at all costs everything that despises and rejects them.

Reverence is more than just love. It includes appreciation for the qualities children possess (which we ourselves have lost), readiness to rediscover their

value, and the humility to learn from them. Reverence is the willingness to accept childhood for its
own sake, and children for who they really are. It is,
as Mumia Abu-Jamal writes, the recognition that they
"show us with their innocence and clarity the very
face of God in human form, by which I simply mean
that they mirror the greatest good we can conceive
of…Don't you feel that when you look into the face
of a child?"

Reverence is trust, too, as we see in the Jewish
midrash which says that when God was bargaining
with the people of Israel he refused to give them the
Torah until they could guarantee its safekeeping.
First they offered God their eldest, but he held them
insufficient. Then they offered him their prophets,
but he held them insufficient too. Only when they
offered God their children did he give in: "They are
certainly good guarantors. For their sake I give you
the Torah."

Finally, reverence is an attitude of deep respect, as
expressed by the following words of my grandfather:

> It is children who lead us to the truth. We are not
> worthy to educate even one of them. Our lips are
> unclean; our dedication is not wholehearted. Our

truthfulness is partial; our love divided. Our kindness is not without motives. We ourselves are not yet free of lovelessness, possessiveness, and selfishness. Only wise men and saints – only those who stand as children before God – are really fit to live and work with children.

Few of us count ourselves wise men or saints. Yet that is exactly why the basis of education must not only be knowledge and understanding, but reverence as well. In Erich Maria Remarque's novel *The Road Back*, written shortly after World War I, there is a passage that illustrates this belief in an unforgettable way. The speaker is Ernst, a veteran of combat in the trenches:

> Morning comes. I go to my class. There sit the little ones with folded arms. In their eyes is still all the shy astonishment of the childish years. They look up at me so trustingly, so believingly – and suddenly I get a spasm over the heart.
>
> Here I stand before you, one of the hundreds of thousands of bankrupt men in whom the war destroyed every belief and almost every strength. Here I stand before you, and see how much more alive, how much more rooted in life you are than I. Here I stand and must now be your teacher and

guide. What should I teach you? Shall I tell you that in twenty years you will be dried-up and crippled, your freest impulses maimed and pressed mercilessly into the selfsame mold? Should I tell you that all learning, all culture, all science is nothing but hideous mockery, so long as mankind makes war in the name of God and humanity with gas, iron, explosive and fire? What should I teach you then, you little creatures who alone have remained unspotted by the terrible years?

What am I able to teach you then? Should I tell you how to pull the string of a hand grenade, how to best throw it at a human being? Should I show you how to stab a man with a bayonet, how to fell him with a club, how to slaughter him with a spade? Should I demonstrate how best to aim a rifle at such an incomprehensible miracle as a breathing breast, a living heart? Should I explain to you what tetanus is, what a broken spine is, and what a shattered skull? Should I mimic how a man with a stomach wound will groan, how one with a lung wound gurgles and one with a head wound whistles? More I do not know. More I have not learned.

Should I take you to the brown-and-green map there, move my finger across it and tell you that here love was murdered? Should I explain to you that the books you hold in your hands are but nets with which men design to snare your simple souls, to entangle you in the undergrowth of fine phrases and the barbed wire of falsified ideas?

I stand here before you, a polluted, a guilty man and can only implore you ever to remain as you are, never to suffer the bright light of your childhood to be misused as a blow flame of hate. About your brows still blows the breath of innocence. How then should I presume to teach you? Behind me, still pursuing, are the bloody years. How then can I venture among you? Must I not first become a child again myself?

I feel a cramp begin to spread through me, as if I were turning to stone, as if I were crumbling away. I lower myself slowly into the chair and realize that I cannot stay here any longer. I try to take hold of something but cannot. Then after a time that has seemed to me endless, the catalepsy relaxes. I stand up. "Children," I say with difficulty, "you may go now. There will be no school today."

The little ones look at me to make sure I am not joking. I nod once again. "Yes, that is right – go and play today – the whole day. Go and play in the wood, or with your dogs and your cats, you need not come back till tomorrow."

With a clatter they toss their pencil boxes into their satchels, and twittering and breathless they scurry off...

As I go to the station, a couple of little girls with smeary mouths and flying hair ribbons come running out from the neighboring house. They have just been burying a dead mole in the garden, so they tell me, and have said a prayer for him. Then they curtsey and shake hands with me. *"Auf Wiedersehen, Herr Lehrer."*

Try doing something similar in a real classroom, and one would be questioned, if not fired. But the point, as Remarque makes clear, is not the incident itself. What is vital here is that the heart of a man is touched by a spirit our age has completely lost. He recognizes, when faced with innocence and vulnerability, honesty and spontaneity, that the only fitting response is reverence.

The idea of the child as teacher, though not an uncommon one, always deserves rediscovery. It is the logical consequence of a reverent approach to children. But when the child is hindered or disabled, it takes on special significance. Hence the inclusion of these thoughts from former U.S. Attorney General

Ramsey Clark, a close friend and fellow peace activist who is also the father of a remarkable woman:

> Ronda was our first child and an astonishingly beautiful baby. Her first year seemed normal to us and to her pediatrician. Before Ronda was two, however, we began a long hegira through the medical establishment seeking a diagnosis and prescription for Ronda's slowness to talk. We journeyed for several years to see different specialists where Ronda was subject to all kinds of testing. Often, diagnoses were diametrically opposed. (Further observation and testing disclosed some retardation and mild epilepsy.)
>
> As Ronda approached school age, we were anxious to provide her with the best opportunity available for schooling. Public schools and private institutions were not able to offer any help. Institutions that provided education for deaf people were not able to deal with multiple handicaps...
>
> There have been many problems over the years in and out of various treatment facilities. It has meant a lot of adjusting for Ronda and for us. But through it all Ronda has always been energetic and has learned steadily, if not easily. She has developed a vocabulary of several thousand words. She

can write short, simple letters. Her sign language is
almost too fast for the human eye. She gives her
mother poor grades for sign language and consid-
ers her father a dunce. She herself has an incredible
memory...

We have long since stopped worrying about
why Ronda cannot hear or understand as we do
and simply wonder at her wisdom, goodness, and
the joy she brings.

Entering the conference room in the modest suite
where Ramsey practices law, the first person you may
see is Ronda at the table, crayon in hand. It is a star-
tling and beautiful scene, unlike anything I've seen in
any other office in New York. Ramsey explains:

> She is not only good company, but a source of
> constant surprise. She enjoys any task at any time
> and is always ready to come or go. Above all,
> Ronda is our teacher. Through her we have
> learned what is really important in life: being to-
> gether and helping each other, the beauty of
> gentleness and patience, the futility of material
> things, the absurdity of fame and personal credit,
> and the harm that comes from selfishness. Our
> daughter has taught us the essential role of love in
> any worthwhile life.

While Ramsey's love for Ronda reveals his humility – an essential part of reverence – it reflects another attitude that is equally rare: the belief that every child has been placed in the world with a purpose and a plan. In an age when people are often assessed in terms of their worth – that is, by intelligence and attractiveness, if not portfolios and bank accounts – there are many for whom this is no longer a self-evident truth. But if we truly love children, we will welcome them all, regardless of their color or capabilities, their family arrangement or their class.

Sadly, the state of our culture is such that we not only sideline countless children but destroy millions more, ensuring the avoidance of those we have decided we do not really want. Many, in all fairness, feel that abortion is akin to murder; I, for one, see it as the ultimate irreverence. But even if one feels (as I do) that the practice is wrong, what is to be gained by attacking those who defend it? Shouldn't we work instead toward the day when no woman feels pressed to resort to it? More than that, shouldn't we hope that all those who are burdened might find healing from their pain?

Dorothy Day, the legendary pacifist and founder of the Catholic Worker, had an abortion in her bohemian days but later gave birth to a daughter, Tamar, and was able to write, "Even the most hardened, the most irreverent, is awed by the stupendous fact of creation. No matter how cynically or casually the worldly may treat the birth of a child, it remains spiritually and physically a tremendous event."

Tamar's birth changed her mother's life, and indeed, every child has such transformative power. This is true even of the stillborn child, or the child who dies as an infant. The death of one of Leo Tolstoy's children, for example, brought healing (at least temporarily) to his famously contentious marriage. Reflecting on the experience afterward, in a letter to a friend, he wrote:

> Our child lived so that those of us who were around him would be inspired by the same love; so that in leaving us and going home to God, who is Love itself, we are drawn all the closer to each other. My wife and I were never so close to each other as now, and we never before felt in ourselves such a need for love, nor such an aversion to any discord or any evil.

I myself sensed something of this as a child, in the way my parents were affected by a similar event in their marriage. My sister Marianne, who died when I was six, lived only twenty-four hours, but became an important part of my life. Two days before the baby's birth, my mother suffered near-fatal heart failure, and it was only by a miracle that she survived delivery at the primitive hospital in the Paraguayan village where we lived.

As a pastor, too, I have seen how every child, no matter how brief its stay, can transform us, if only we allow it to. I experienced this most strikingly a few years ago, in the arrival of a baby whose twin died before birth. If nothing else, the event (told here by the father, Joe) shows that even a stillborn child can help us to discover the meaning of reverence.

> Shortly after we found out that only one of our twins was going to make it, Deborah and I made an appointment with our obstetrician, just to sit together and talk about what had happened and what lay ahead of us. He said he didn't know why the baby died, and that we might never know... One comment in particular touched us: "When the dead baby arrives, it might be discolored, floppy,

shriveled; but we won't care what it looks like. To us, it will be beautiful." Then, to Deborah: "It was a living soul inside of you. You felt it move, you talked to it, you loved it like only a mother can, and you will love it no matter what it looks like." He encouraged her to hold both babies.

Facing the prospect of burying a little child of our own was unimaginably difficult at first, particularly when we thought of how trying the birth would be. But over the next days we began to realize how precious that day would be. We realized that there would be very little time to see and hold the child, and very little we would be able to do for it. So we began to look forward to it, hard as we knew it would be...

When the moment of birth finally came, Lloyd, our living baby, was the first to arrive. He lay there on Deborah's arm as the contractions continued for a few more minutes, and we waited nervously, preparing for a long struggle. In the end it all went smoothly, and suddenly the doctor was announcing that the other baby had arrived.

Loren, our beloved second twin, was beautifully formed, though his bones had become very soft, and his skull had almost entirely disintegrated. But that didn't matter. A small knit hat was soon holding it in place, and I laid his tiny hand on one of my fingers, and sat with him like that for fifteen or twenty minutes. Loren had the same little white spots on his nose as Lloyd.

After the nurse cleaned Loren's body, his Grandma made hand and footprints, and we placed him in a tiny white casket that was waiting next door. Deborah clipped a tiny lock of his hair and taped it to his birth record, and then dressed him in a little nightgown and wrapped him in a blanket.

Later we laid Lloyd next to his brother. He had been fussing, but once the two of them were lying side by side, he settled right down and went to sleep. He must have known this was the last time they would be together. Then we put Loren back into his casket, and placed his perfect little hand around a bouquet.

By this time our other children came to see their two baby brothers. We had told them what had happened, but didn't know what to expect. They crowded around the tiny casket, looking in total silence. They didn't seem at all puzzled by his appearance, or afraid...

Loren never breathed, never opened his eyes, never made a sound. He died before he left his mother's womb. We'll never know what caused his death, nor exactly when he died. But we do know that Loren was entrusted to us, even if briefly, and given into our care. And we know with a certainty that God had a purpose for this, and that he accomplished that purpose.

People who don't know better might be tempted to say that Loren never lived. But not us. He changed our lives forever. Even his healthy brother will always remember his first playmate, and will always go through life with an awareness of his twin. Hardly a day goes by without him telling us that his brother is "watching me in heaven." And for that reason alone we know Loren's life was not in vain.

9. Learning to Let Go

You may house their bodies but not their souls...
which you cannot visit even in your dreams.

KAHLIL GIBRAN

It is no small thing to bring up even one child – to clear the shallows of childhood, to navigate the rocky passages of adolescence, and to steer him safely down river into the harbor of adulthood. But the journey does not end there: after raising our children and setting them on their feet, we must let them go. In any case – and most of us wouldn't have it any other way – children do grow up to lead lives of their own. Our primary task, then, must be to raise them in such a way that when they go out into what

Pestalozzi calls "the stream of the world," they are strong enough to make their own decisions, and to hold to them. Viktor Frankl, a survivor of Auschwitz best known for his book *Man's Search for Meaning*, writes:

> Research on heredity has shown how high is the degree of human freedom in the face of predisposition. As for environment, we know that it does not make a person, but that everything depends on what he makes of it, on his attitude toward it. But there is another element: decision. We ultimately decide for ourselves! And in the end, education must always be education toward the ability to decide.

While inspiring, Frankl's advice is easier to reflect on than to actually practice. Because if there's anything almost every one of us succumbs to again and again, it is the temptation to make decisions for our children rather than guiding them to decide for themselves. And it is no help that adolescence, during which this parenting skill is needed most, is also the time we're most concerned about their ability to stand on their own.

A young adult's world consists of a jumble of tensions: an insistence on being left alone and a need to be included, a longing for freedom and a readiness for responsibility, a feeling of invincibility and a fear of failure, a distaste for conformity and a desire to fit in. Aside from all this there are the continual frictions that arise from peer pressure on the one hand and parental authority on the other. Is it any wonder that so few teenagers escape from the battle unscathed at least in some way, and that more are not wounded for life? It is certainly the reason that many parents are so reluctant to see how they might fare on their own.

A friend who's always e-mailing me things sent me a riddle the other day about the difference between a mother and a Rottweiler (answer: the dog eventually lets go). As a joke, it's momentarily funny; as a fact of life, it is less so. For one thing, to clamp down on a child is to crush him, and even if he comes away looking unscathed, the bruises will show up sooner or later. Good intentions make no difference. Most teens I know, while receptive enough to the idea of boundaries, submit to them primarily to avoid the consequences. They resist the very thought that they are there because they need protection.

Ed, a guidance counselor I know, says that among the teens he has worked with, the one who slid farthest and fastest from their parents' values were the ones who were overprotected and never given the slightest chance to try out their wings:

> One young man, Nick, played along with his parents as long as he was in high school: he was a model kid – polite and kind. But you should have seen him once he left home – hard drinking, sex-crazed, and totally unable to control himself...
>
> Another student, Cara, felt her parents didn't care about her as a person, but just how she reflected on them as parents. She kept her rebellion under wraps most of the time, but even then she seethed. She was convinced she'd never match her father's ideal of a "nice" girl, and the stricter they got with her, the more she lashed out at them. In the end, she ran off to relatives in California...

Surely neither of these teenagers was any worse than their peers. But in both situations, because their parents denied them the opportunity to make mistakes, their most strenuous efforts to bring them up successfully ended miserably. In Nick's case, the pattern was classic: the carefully groomed child submitted as long as he had to, but once circumstances pulled him from the control of his parents, there was nothing they could do – and nothing he could, either, since he didn't have a leg to stand on. With Cara the problem was familiar too: in forgetting that their child was an individual in her own right, her parents seemed to act less out of genuine concern than possessiveness, and ended up having to battle with the justifiable protests of a daughter who refused to be owned.

But what is the alternative? According to my grandfather, freedom: "It is not the over-protection of anxious adults, but trust in a watchful care beyond our power that gives a child a sure instinct in dangerous situations. In freedom lies the best protection for a child."

Freedom, of course, does not mean license to do whatever one wants. The youthful desire for independence is natural enough, yet children must be taught that it always comes with corresponding responsibilities. To give even the most mature adoles-

cent free rein is to ask for trouble. As the following
anecdote from Jean, a neighbor, shows, it is also a
disservice:

> I was raised in a very permissive home. This was
> intentional on my parents' part. They didn't agree
> with what they felt was repressive in the way my
> mother was brought up, and decided it would be
> quite different for their children.
>
> My father wanted me to know that there is "no
> such thing as absolute truth," and he abhorred
> people who were so narrow-minded. Once he il-
> lustrated his point this way: If a new bridge is be-
> ing built connecting Brooklyn and Manhattan, it's
> great for the people who drive over the bridge but
> terrible for those who have to give up their family
> homes to make it possible. Everything is relative,
> good for some people, bad for others...
>
> The way it worked in my life was that I could do
> whatever I wanted to. My father said, "When you
> touch the stove, you find out what heat is. You will
> learn about life from your own experiences."
>
> I wasn't expected to do anything around the
> house. My mother often complained about how
> messy my room was, but nothing was ever done to
> change it. I remember one time when I announced

that I was leaving home and my father said, "OK, I'll help you pack."

I'm sure I did have some wonderful childhood experiences; it's just that the idea of childlike innocence wasn't regarded very highly in our home. Instead, my parents taught me about drinking – the different kinds of whisky and liquor, etc. – and how to smoke. We always had the latest copy of Playboy magazine in the bathroom. If I stayed out late or didn't want to come home at night, that was also okay...By the time I was a young adult I had experimented with just about everything that came my way.

While many teenagers might regard such a lenient setting as the ideal home, Jean says it wasn't. Already timid and painfully shy, the complete absence of limits or boundaries only heightened her feelings of insecurity and made her more unhappy and even depressed:

True joy was unknown to me. I was empty inside, and desperate to find something to hold on to... Now, as a mother of teenagers myself, I have great difficulty helping them. I don't want the same void for them. I feel their need of clear guidelines, yet I am often simply unable to provide them. I'm still searching for that bottom line or ground myself. It's like I am permanently on shifting sand.

Clearly, parenting is often somewhat of a balancing act, and it is as easy to err on the side of permissiveness as on the side of authoritarianism. Yet there is a third way, described by the father below, who has a definite sense of the goals he has set for his children yet is still open to growing with them and learning from them:

> The older my children get, the more plainly I see the futility of merely trying to keep them on the "right" track, rather than guiding them in such a way that they can hone their own inner sense of direction. If I am always nudging them as soon as they stray the slightest bit, they will never know what it is to recognize their errors on their own...Of course, that always takes a lot of patience – not to mention trust in the power of their own consciences.

Speaking from my own experience as a teen, I do not know what I would have done without the trust my parents showed in me and my siblings, even though I know there were plenty of times when we frustrated or disappointed them. And rather than distancing themselves from us over those incidents or taking them personally, my parents used them as occasions for deepening our relationship as a family. My father used to tell us – and this has always stayed with me – "I would rather be betrayed a dozen times than live in mistrust." There is nothing that draws parent and child so close as such loyalty.

Obviously we must have confidence in our goals, quite apart from what our children think. We must know what we want and do not want for them. But it is one thing to be confident and another to be over-bearing. Therefore it is vital, whenever things come to a head, not only to set things back on track, but also (once that has been done) to trust in the good intentions of our children, to forgive them, and to move on. Every one of us was a teenager once, and each of us has made poor choices or done things we regret – and just as often defended them. Why should we insist on holding our sons and daughters to a higher standard?

Perhaps too many of us react rather than respond to the challenges our children present us with. Jumping angrily into the fray on one occasion and turning a blind eye on the next, we sigh defensively about how times have changed. Blumhardt writes:

> Too many parents demand excessive submission from their adolescent children; they put pressure on them even in the most trifling matters and treat them as if they were still young. They are intolerant; they correct, punish, and find fault with everything...But there is never an atmosphere of friendliness. Such parents are constantly after their children and give them no independence. Is it any wonder that their children's greatest desire is to escape the house?

In my experience, this problem is more common than one might think. It arises from the unhealthy emotionalism that is so often mistaken for love. Again and again I have seen how parents hang on to their adolescent children with possessive affection – that is, with hopes of being loved in return – and when their efforts are resisted or spurned, their feelings are hurt. The results are almost always disastrous. If only these parents were able to put themselves in their children's shoes, rather than complaining about how unreachable they are, they might find the perspective necessary for arriving at a common understanding. To quote my grandfather:

> Some children are brought up in an unbelievably free way and are, by my standards, awfully cheeky and naughty. But I think that too much freedom is better than the slavish fear that makes a child's parents the last ones he'll turn to…Happy those children who have a mother to whom they can pour out their hearts and always count on her understanding, and a father in whose strength and loyalty they are so confident that they seek his advice and help all their lives. Many people long to be such parents to their children, and could be, if only they possessed enough wisdom and love.

It is rare that a child cannot be reached at some level – if not by listening to him and trying to understand the reason for his silence, his rebellion, or his distress, then at least by acknowledging his hurt. Flat rules and prohibitions, of course, are seldom a help. Neither are long talks, probing questions, and attempts to make a child "open up." Respect, however, is always in order, because it almost always inspires respect in turn. Barbara, a British friend, remembers:

> One time when I was really down and tied up in
> knots, Dad took a day off from work and took me
> on a long walk through the woods, after which we
> had a late lunch at a country inn. He didn't try to
> make me talk and certainly did not attempt to give
> me any kind of advice. We just spent the day to-
> gether. But I will never forget that day. It really
> made me feel special inside.
>
> Some time later I went through a period of real
> depression, and he bought two tickets for a play at
> a London theater. It was just me and him...Looking
> back after all these years I'm sure he never really
> knew how or why I was hurting so much inside.
> I'm also sure that he never knew how much both
> gestures still mean to me.

For children and teens in general, this love is the
greatest security we can provide. And as Barbara's
recollection shows, it need not even be verbalized.
When the chips are down, it is always our deeds, not
our words, that prove how much another person
means to us.

It is the same with respect to a child's future. As
we have already seen, possessive attempts at control-

ling a child will always backfire, while the lack of any guidance at all may leave him feeling that neither his goals, nor he himself, really matter. But when a child feels that his future is important to us, not just because we are his parents, but because we care for him on his own terms, even the most difficult situation can be addressed. Love will always find a way.

At one level or another, every one of us wants our children to follow in our footsteps, at least as far as our basic values are concerned. When they lack direction, we feel the need to channel their energies toward a positive end; when they are confused or insecure, we want to offer guidance and support. When, as young adults, they finally cut the apron strings, we are tempted to tell them that they must simultaneously tie themselves to new obligations. All that is perfectly natural.

Yet if we love our children, we will never coerce them or make claims on them. We will see ourselves not as their owners or masters, but as their guardians. Finally, guided by the spirit of reverence that sees in each human being a unique creature that possesses his own innate worth, we will never forget that every child is (to borrow from my grandfather again) a "thought in the mind of God." And following that, we will always keep in mind the vital necessity of his finding the specific and personal meaning that life has for him, and him alone.

While such an understanding of children might seem conventional enough, it carries a deep responsibility. And this is especially true in our time, when for all the talk about the importance of the individual, the homogenization of the culture has leveled society as never before, and made us all far more similar than we might like to admit. Choose the circle you like: everyone is wearing the same clothes, eating at the same chains, reading the same books and magazines, watching the same shows, talking about the same celebrity scandals, the same disasters, the same political events. We have been made to feel we are our own masters, yet we cannot even think for ourselves. Foerster suggests why this is so:

> Without an ideal of personal character to fortify us, we fall prey only too easily to our social instincts; that is, to our fear of men, our ambition, our social desire to please, and all other herd instincts. Group life, the traffic of people, collective organization,

and the strength and expression of public opinion, have become greater and greater, while the organization of the personal inner life has become weaker and weaker, and the true individual is smothered in the midst of all the individualism.

If we are truly committed to bringing up our children as individuals – to raising young women and men who have strength to defy the largest crowd – we will not only change the way we treat them but also start believing in them. Instead of worrying about whether they feel comfortable and well-adjusted or overburdened and stressed-out, we will rouse them to become more responsible, persevering, and selfless. Instead of just "being there" for them in a passive sort of way and hoping that, somewhere along the way, they'll grow up and "find themselves," we will stimulate them and set them challenges and goals.

Finally, even if we recognize that what our children do with their lives is their decision, we will love them enough to nudge them from the cozy nest we have feathered for them. In short, we will help them to see that there is more to life than finding a "good" job and leading the "good" life – and that true fulfillment is found only when we begin to look further than our own comfort.

Too many young people today are suffocating in bottomless heaps of material wealth, in boredom, in isolation, and in artificial environments that purport to give them happiness but deaden them by shielding them from the real world. And it is no wonder. Young people don't want comfort and security. They want self-sacrifice and risks. And when they don't want that, they at very least want to give. Dave, a friend and pastor in Littleton, Colorado, who regularly involves his youth group in volunteer activities, says:

> Kids are so hungry to contribute, to do something creative, to give...and once you can get them to start looking out for others, they survive. Service isn't comfort. But it gives you a purpose in life, and it forces you to stop thinking about yourself...
>
> If you don't live for others, you end up being consumed with yourself. Once you start giving, though, your emotional needs will eventually take care of themselves.

As it is, children and young adults are often made to feel they have little or nothing to offer. Yet if we would give them sufficient opportunities, I am convinced that, like Dave, we would find out how much they yearn to do more than look out for their own skins. No matter the attitudes and concerns they exhibit on the surface, young adults everywhere long to contribute to their fellow human beings, to make a difference, and to change the world.

It is precisely these opportunities – the chances we offer our children to give of themselves and to grow beyond themselves – that will provide them with the knowledge that they do indeed have something to give, and that it is their duty to give it. And from this knowledge they will eventually gain the sense, as Frankl puts it, that the question they ought to be asking is not, "What is the meaning of my life?" but "What is life asking of me?" Frankl continues:

> It may also be put this way...Life is putting its problems to us, and it is up to us to respond to these questions by being responsible; we can only answer to life by answering for our life.

Raising children conscientiously, yet letting them go; protecting them, yet encouraging self-sacrifice;

guiding them, yet preparing them to swim against the stream – all these paradoxical dimensions of parenting are touched on in the following story.

When Uwe Holmer was fourteen, in 1943, the patriotic teen was an energetic member of the local Hitler Youth. One day his mother found a copy of *The Black Corps,* the magazine of the SS, in his room. When Uwe came home, she took time to talk with him and begged him never to join the SS. "But, Mama, they are the toughest soldiers. They fight to the bitter end." "Yes," she answered, "and they are the ones who shoot prisoners and Jews. Is that the sort of organization you want to live and die for?" Uwe never forgot her question, or the look on her face.

A year later, as Germany grew desperate to hold off defeat, the army began accepting fifteen-year-olds for military service. All one hundred boys in Uwe's chapter of the Hitler Youth volunteered for the SS. Uwe refused. The leader of the group called him in and ordered him to join; his papers were filled out and ready to sign. Still Uwe refused. Next he was humiliated in front of the entire chapter, and all his privileges revoked, but he stood his ground. As he said later: "I am thankful to my mother…her courage in confronting me strengthened my conviction to live for what I knew was right."

After the war, in East Germany, Uwe married, became a pastor, and founded a Christian community for epileptics and mentally disabled adults. Over the years, the Holmers suffered repeated harassment on account of their pastoral activities, especially under the government of Erich Honecker. Yet after the 1989 fall of the Berlin Wall, when Honecker fled office as one of Europe's most hated men, it was Uwe and his wife who took the ailing despot in – despite death threats and constant loud protests outside their house.

To me, the most striking thing about Uwe's story is its matter-of-factness. Yes, he had the guts to defy authority in a time and place where disobedience often cost a man his life. Years later, misunderstood and ridiculed, he withstood public opinion in defense of a broken fugitive who had nowhere to go. But Uwe's actions say as much about the power of his upbringing as they do about his heroism.

For whatever else a childhood is, one thing is constant: it is the hearth, the gathering place of life's first and most indelible memories – the unalterable frame for all the experiences that accompany us through life. And thus in the end, the task of bringing up our children is not only a question of effective parenting, and even less one of educational insights, theories, or ideals. Perhaps it is mostly a matter of the love we give them, and the memories engendered by that love, which has power to awaken the same even years down the road. As Dostoyevsky reminds us in the final pages of *The Brothers Karamazov:*

> You must know that there is nothing higher and stronger and more wholesome for life in the future than some good memory, especially a memory of childhood, of home. People talk to you a great deal about education. But some good, sacred memory preserved from childhood – that is perhaps the best education. For if a man has only one good memory left in his heart, even that may keep him from evil...And if he carries many such memories with him into life, he is safe for the end of his days.

Afterword

*There is never time to say our last word –
the last word of our love or remorse.*

JOSEPH CONRAD

It is one thing to read (or write) about bringing up children, and quite another to actually do it. Words are easy to come by; so are anecdotes and suggestions. Yet without deeds, the soundest educational theory is useless, as is the most trustworthy parental instinct. When all is said and done, we must put away our books and go out to find the children who need our love.

In our country alone there are thousands, possibly millions, of children who have never felt the tenderness that every child deserves; who go to bed hungry and lonely and cold; who, though housed by the parents who conceived them, know little of the love of true parenthood. Add to that the numberless children for whom such love can never become a reality, even if desired, because the cruel cycle of poverty and crime has landed father or mother or both behind bars. Still, we cannot despair.

If only a fraction of us who have resources were willing to commit our energy and time to helping one endangered child, even our own child, many might be saved. And even if our kindness takes the shape of the smallest, most negligible act, it will, like every deed of love, never be wasted. Invisible as it might be on its own, it will still carry meaning; together with others it may have power to change the world.

Such promises might ring hollow, but that is not because they are empty. It is because we have forgotten that the tie that binds one generation to the next means far more than the sharing of blood. As humanity's oldest and strongest bond, the love between a parent and a child is a gift for the future – an inheritance for posterity.

Unfortunately, the wreckage that so often passes for family life these days leads some people to be fatalistic about the way things are. But why should these pessimists have the last word? Dorothy Day writes:

> The sense of futility is one of the greatest evils of the day...People say, "What can one person do? What is the sense of our small effort?" They cannot see that we can only lay one brick at a time, take one step at a time; we can be responsible only for the one action of the present moment.

This wisdom – the importance of living in the present – is another of the many lessons children could teach us, if we were willing to lay aside our adult "solutions" long enough to hear theirs. As Assata Shakur recently admonished a crowd of activists bent on changing the world:

> We need to include children, to make space for them, to let them be part of the social transformation...Children are the most important source of optimism on this planet. But we've tended not to listen to them, not to pay attention to the wisdom that comes out of their mouths.

It is often said that children "are our future" or that

we must educate them "for the future." While the sentiment is understandable, it is also a limiting one. There is nothing like the joy of anticipation: of watching one's children grow, marking the development of their personalities, and wondering and waiting to see what they will become. But as long as we have children entrusted to our care, we cannot forget that the demands they make on us must be answered in the present.

There is always a tomorrow, but how can we be sure it will be ours? There are always new chances, but how many will we let become missed opportunities and regrets? For the sake of a child, are we ready to drop everything – not begrudgingly, but with joy? If we cannot answer these questions, perhaps we have not learned the most important lesson of all: that whatever a child needs in the way of guidance, security, and love, he needs now.

> Many things can wait. Children cannot.
> Today their bones are being formed, their blood
> is being made, their senses are being developed.
> To them we cannot say "tomorrow."
> Their name is today.
>
> *Gabriela Mistral*

Notes and Sources

Page x. The West Indian journalist is Peter Noel, in his article "If a cop kills my son..." in *The Village Voice,* April 4–10, 2000.

Page 1. Susan and Nick are based on a couple described in Sylvia Ann Hewlett and Cornel West, *The War Against Parents* (Houghton Mifflin, 1998) 26–27.

Page 3–4. Statistics on murder, homelessness, divorce, etc., are taken from Johann Christoph Arnold, *A Little Child Shall Lead Them* (Plough, 1996); James Garbarino, *Raising Children in a Socially Toxic Environment* (Jossey-Bass, 1995); Michael and Diane Medved, *Saving Childhood* (HarperCollins, 1998); and the websites of the Children's Defense Fund and UNICEF.

Page 5. For Madeleine Albright's comments on *60 Minutes,* see *The Plough* (Special Issue on Iraq, May 1997) 10.

Page 6–8. The extended quote from Mumia Abu-Jamal is condensed from "Year of the Child," an unpublished essay he sent to the author in August 1999.

Page 11. The comparisons between war deaths and domestic murders and suicides are based on statistics from Superior Court Judge Charles Gill (Litchfield, Connecticut) in a talk at Deer Spring School, Norfolk, CT, May 11, 1996.

Page 12. The anecdote about the policeman and drug dealers is from James Garbarino, *Raising Children in a Socially Toxic Environment* (Jossey-Bass, 1995) 66–67.

Page 13. The closing words from Mumia Abu-Jamal are from *The Plough* 48 (Summer 1996) 19.

Page 14. The opening excerpt is from Martha Beck, *Expecting Adam* (Random House, 1999) 203–207.

Page 23. Robert Coles's words are quoted in William Bausch, *Becoming A Man* (Twenty-Third Publications, 1988) 194–195.

Page 24. The material from Mother Teresa is from Teresa de Bertodano, comp., *Daily Readings with Mother Teresa* (HarperCollins, 1993) 62–63.

Page 31. The Kenyan saying is from *New Internationalist* (August 1999) 24.

Page 34. The quote from Johann Christoph Blumhardt is from his *Thoughts About Children* (Plough, 1980) 6.

Page 35. The quote from Friedrich Froebel is from his *Education of Man* (Appleton, 1900) 55.

Page 35. The statistics re: the abolition of recess in American public schools is from Anna Mulrine, "What's Your

Favorite Class?" in *U.S. News and World Report,* May 1, 2000, 50–52.

Page 38. The quote from Jonathan Kozol is from his book *Ordinary Resurrections: Children in the Years of Hope* (Crown, 2000) 119.

Page 40–41. The quote about the difficulty of getting into private schools is from the Clyde Haberman's Metro Matters column, "Rat Race Intrudes at Age Five" in *The New York Times,* March 10, 2000.

Page 42. Jonathan Kozol's words are from *The Plough* 47 (Spring 1996) 12–13.

Page 43–44. The comments from John Taylor Gatto are quoted in Scott Savage, ed., *The Plain Reader: Essays on Making a Simple Life* (Ballantine, 1998) 213.

Page 46. The lines from Jane Tyson Clement are from an unpublished poem, "Child, though I take your hand" (1965).

Page 55. The anecdote about the use of standardized reading scores in Texas is from *BLU* 7 (Special Issue on Women in Struggle) 3.

Page 56. Janusz Korczak's words are quoted in *The Plough* 48 (Summer 1996) 5.

Page 58. Anthony Bloom's words are from his book, *Beginning to Pray* (Paulist, 1970) 5.

Page 59. Friedrich Froebel's thoughts are from his book *The Education of Man* (Appleton, 1900) 124.

Page 63–64. For more about Janusz Korczak, see Betty Jean Lifton's biography, *The King of Children* (St. Martins, 1997).

Page 65–68. The material on Tokyo teens is from Howard W. French, "Dropouts' Career in Japan," in *The New York Times,* March 5, 2000.

Page 69–70. The piece about "Generation Why?" is from Marcy Musgrave, "Generation Has Some Questions," *Dallas Morning News,* May 2, 1999.

Page 72–73. The quote from Fyodor Dostoyevsky is from *The Brothers Karamazov* (Random House, 1950) 383.

Page 73. Mary Pipher's words are quoted in Deirdre Donahue, "No-nonsense therapist takes society to task," *USA Today,* April 9, 1996.

Page 74–76. Barbara Kingsolver's piece originally appeared as an op-ed piece, "Either life is precious or it's not," in the *Los Angeles Times,* May 2, 1999.

Page 77–78. Johann Christoph Blumhardt's words are from his book, *Thoughts About Children* (Plough, 1980) 28–29.

Page 78. Assata Shakur's words are from a talk she gave at the International Youth Conference in Havana, Cuba, August 1997.

Page 85. Malcolm X's words are taken from his *Autobiography* (Ballantine, 1992) 411.

Page 101. The statistics on increased Ritalin use are from Susan Okie, "Preschoolers rush to join Prozac nation," a *Washington Post* piece reprinted in the *Guardian Weekly*, March 2–8, 2000; see also similar articles on Ritalin in *The New York Times* (Robert Pear, "Curbing Use of Psychiatric Drugs for Children" and "Widespread Support for Clinton on Ritalin," both March 20, 2000; and Erica Good, "Sharp Rise Found in Psychiatric Drugs for the Very Young," March 23, 2000).

Page 102–103. The material from Peter Breggin is from a March 29, 2000 interview with epidemiologist Michael Savage posted on NewsMax.com.

Page 103–104. Regarding "convenience" abortions, see *The British Medical Journal,* March 23, 1996, 312:727–728.

Page 104. The material from Friedrich Foerster is quoted in Johann Christoph Arnold, *Seeking Peace* (Plough, 1998) 67–68.

Page 108. "Worrying statistics" are widely available; take for example, the fact that the suicide rate among children from 10–14 years of age has risen 109% since 1980 (Paul Zielhaber, "Two Boys Tell friends Goodbye...", *The New York Times,* May 3, 2000); or the fact that despite dropping US juvenile crime and arrest rates, the number of prison inmates under 18 has more than doubled since 1985 (Anjetta McQueen, "Youth Imprisonment Doubles," AP newswire, February 28, 2000). Forty-two states have revised their juvenile crime statutes since 1992 to make them harsher, with the result that today's teen convicts tend to serve much longer sentences than yesterday's did. See *ColorLines Magazine,* Winter 1999/ 2000 (Special Issue: The War on Youth).

Page 115–116. Janusz Korczak's thoughts on the "good" child are from Sandra Joseph, ed., *A Voice for the Child: The Inspirational Words of Janusz Korczak* (Harper Collins, 1999) 126.

Page 116. The quote from Thomas Lickona is from his book *Raising Good Children* (Bantam, 1994) 125.

Page 133. Hermann Hesse's words are from *Vivos Vocos,* March 1919, as translated and quoted in Eberhard Arnold, *Salt and Light* (Plough, 1997) 48.

Page 134–135. Ari Goldman's words are from his book *The Search for God at Harvard* (Ballantine Books, 1991) 57–58.

Page 136. Mumia Abu-Jamal's words are from *The Plough 48* (Summer 1996) 19.

Page 136. The source of the midrash regarding children and the Torah is Marian Wright Edelman, as quoted in *The Plough 48* (Summer 1996) 16.

Page 136–137. Eberhard Arnold's words are paraphrased from his book *Children's Education in Community* (Plough, 1976) 13–14.

Page 137–140. The extended quote by Erich Maria Remarque is from his book *The Road Back* (Fawcett, 1998) 252–255.

Page 144. The quote by Dorothy Day is from Stanley Vishnewski, comp., *Dorothy Day: Meditations* (Newman Press, 1970) 10.

Page 144. The quote by Leo Tolstoy is from a letter (March 31, 1895) in Karl Noetzel, ed., *Leo Tolstoi: Religioese Briefe,* (Gemeinshafts-Verlag Eberhard Arnold, 1923) 20–21.

Page 150. The quote from Viktor Frankl is from his book *The Doctor and the Soul: from Psychotherapy to Logotherapy* (Vintage, 1986) xxv.

Page 153. Eberhard Arnold's words are from his book *Children's Education in Community* (Plough, 1976) 23.

Page 158. Johann Christoph Blumhardt's words are from his book *Thoughts about Children* (Plough, 1980) 23–24.

Page 159. Eberhard Arnold's words are from an undated postcard (probably October 1908) in "The Engagement Letters of Eberhard Arnold and Emmy von Hollander," Vol. VII:281, an unpublished collection in the Bruderhof Archives.

Page 162–163. Friedrich Wilhelm Foerster's words are from an unpublished typescript in the Bruderhof Archives translated from his *Hauptaufgaben der Erziehung* (Herder, 1959).

Page 164. Dave McPherson's words are quoted by Misty Bernall in *She Said Yes* (Plough, 1999) 102–103.

Page 165. The quote from Viktor Frankl is from his book *The Doctor and the Soul: from Psychotherapy to Logotherapy* (Vintage, 1986) xxi.

Page 166–167. Uwe Holmer's story has been widely reported in books, magazines, and on the Internet. The direct quotes are translated from Thomas Lackmann, "Beim Abschied umarmten wir uns" (an interview with Uwe Holmer), *Der Tagesspiegel*, Beilage Weltspiegel Nr. 16860.

Page 168. The quote from Fyodor Dostoyevsky is from *The Brothers Karamazov* (Random House, 1950) 938.

Page 171. The quote from Dorothy Day is from her book, *From Union Square to Rome* (Preservation of the Faith Press, 1938) 127.

Page 171. Assata Shakur's words are from an interview, "Know Thyself," in *BLU* 7 (Special Issue on Women in Struggle) 36.

Page 172. The closing lines by Gabriela Mistral are from a collection of quotations on the website of author Sydney Gurewitz Clemens, an early childhood educator.

Acknowledgments

Dozens of people helped bring this book into print, but I would especially like to thank Ellen, Emmy Maria, Hannah, Charles, Kim, Chris, and the rest of the staff at Plough.

I would also like to thank Mumia Abu-Jamal, Dale Recinella, and Ramsey Clark for their contributions to the book, as well as numerous others whose names have been changed to protect their privacy.

Finally, I thank my wife, Verena. Without her encouragement, *Endangered* could not have been written. And without her knack for catching mistakes everyone else misses, it would be an inferior book.

Acknowledgments are also due the following writers and publishers:

Mitch Albom, for the excerpt from his book *Tuesdays with Morrie: An Old Man, A Young Man, and*

Index

Hardcover, 264 pages.

Seeking Peace
Notes and Conversations along the Way
Johann Christoph Arnold
Preface by Thich Nhat Hanh

For anyone sick of the spiritual soup filling so many bookstore shelves these days, *Seeking Peace* is sure to satisfy a deep hunger. Arnold offers no easy solutions, but also no unrealistic promises. He spells out what peace demands. There is a peace greater than self-fulfillment, he writes. But you won't find it if you go looking for it. It is waiting for everyone ready to sacrifice the search for individual peace, everyone ready to "die to self."

Thomas Howard, St. John's Seminary
Outstanding. The candor, simplicity, and humanity of the whole text, and especially of the anecdotes, should recommend it to an exceedingly wide reading public.

Mairead Maguire, Nobel Peace Prize laureate
Arnold inspires each of us to seek peace within our own lives…His book gives hope that we can indeed find wholeness, happiness, and harmony.

Hardcover, 176 pages.

Why Forgive?
Johann Christoph Arnold

In *Why Forgive?* the reader will meet men and women who have earned the right to talk about the importance of overcoming hurt – and about the peace of mind they have found in doing so. As in life, not every story has a happy ending – a fact Arnold refuses to skirt. The book also addresses the difficulty of forgiving oneself, the temptation to blame God, and the turmoil of those who simply cannot seem to forgive, even though they try. Why forgive? Read these stories, and then decide.

ALA Booklist
A most impressive book…So powerful that tears often impede reading.

Publishers Weekly
Reminds us that to forgive is not to excuse or to anesthetize ourselves from the pain that attends life and love, but rather to enter again into life's fray.

To order, call: 1-800-521-8011 (US) or 0800 018 0799 (UK)

Hardcover, 160 pages,
10 photographs.

She Said Yes
The Unlikely Martyrdom of Cassie Bernall
By Misty Bernall
Foreword by Madeleine L'Engle

Almost everyone who knows anything about the April 1999 massacre at Columbine High School knows about Cassie Bernall, the student who, on being asked whether she believed in God and answering "yes," was shot to death by two crazed classmates. But Cassie's parents knew only too well that behind the image of the smiling saint portrayed by the media was a teenager who worried about her weight, her work, and her chances of finding a boyfriend. It's a story that her mother, Misty Bernall, tells with alarming honesty – and a book everyone who cares about teens needs to read.

People Magazine
Far more complicated and enlightening than the tidy martyrdom imposed on Cassie after her death. A poignant wake-up call to parents.

The Denver Post
A highly personal tale of the perils of parenting, a teenager's search for her identity, and hope during the darkest of days.

Book (incl. CD):
Hardcover, 112 pages.
(CD and cassette also
available separately.)

Sing through the Day
Eighty Songs for Children
Comp. by Marlys Swinger
Illustr. by Nancy and Brenna McKernan

It's all here, from playing with puppies and watching clouds, to celebrating birthdays and dreaming dreams of magic ponies. While the majority of the songs are folk tunes, there are new treasures, too. The lyrics include classic poems from Christina Rossetti, Robert Louis Stevenson, Hans Christian Andersen, and many others. Melodic and simple enough for any child to pick up, each song is presented with piano accompaniment and guitar chords. A FREE sing-along CD is included. Ideal for families, home-schoolers, daycare centers, preschool programs, and elementary grades. Illustrated in full color.

To order, call: 1-800-521-8011 (US) or 0800 018 0799 (UK)